J. F. Ferris

Practical Artificial Incubation

A resumé of the progress made in the past few years in artificial

incubation in this country and Europe

J. F. Ferris

Practical Artificial Incubation
A resumé of the progress made in the past few years in artificial incubation in this country and Europe

ISBN/EAN: 9783337381967

Printed in Europe, USA, Canada, Australia, Japan

Cover: Foto ©Andreas Hilbeck / pixelio.de

More available books at **www.hansebooks.com**

PRACTICAL

Artificial Incubation.

A RESUME OF THE PROGRESS MADE
IN THE PAST FEW YEARS IN ARTIFICIAL
INCUBATION IN THIS COUNTRY AND EUROPE.

WITH DESCRIPTIONS OF A SCORE OF
LEADING INCUBATORS IN SUCCESSUL OPERATION IN
AMERICA AND ENGI

ALSO,

CHAPTERS UPON THE PROPER

Care and Management of the Young Chicks.

BY

J. F. FERRIS,

EDITOR OF "THE POULTRY MONTHLY" AND "THE FANCIERS' WEEKLY."

PROFUSELY ILLUSTRATED.

ALBANY
FERRIS PUBLISHING COMPANY.
1880.

Cordially Yours,
J. F. Ferris.

TO THE THOUSANDS OF

Fanciers and Breeders,

WHO, FOR THE PAST YEAR, HAVE SO HANDSOMELY SUPPORTED ME IN MY EFFORTS TO
ESTABLISH A THOROUGHLY LIVE AND READABLE POULTRY MONTHLY,

This Volume is Respectfully Dedicated, by

THEIR OBEDIENT SERVANT,

J. F. FERRIS.

"It is better that every kind of work, honestly undertaken and discharged, should speak for itself than be spoken for."— CHARLES DICKENS.

INTRODUCTORY.

It is a wise chicken that knows its own mother in these days of "Wooden Hens," "Eclipse Incubators," "Perfect Hatchers," and the score or more of other devices rapidly coming into use to bring forth the downy little creatures! For many years we have prophesied that in a very short time the incubator would entirely revolutionize the poultry interests of this country as well as Europe. That our prophecy is fast being verified, both in this country and in England, even in the year 1880, is rapidly being demonstrated by the score of new machines that are already being operated successfully. Extensive breeders in every part of America are realizing this fact, and in our position as editor of the POULTRY MONTHLY, we are almost daily in receipt of letters asking an opinion of this, that, and the other machine, as well as for facts regarding the successful use of incubators in general. We began the preparation of this work nearly a year ago, but from a pressure of other duties it has been postponed from time to time, and now, after a somewhat hasty preparation, it is placed before the public for what it may be worth.

In compiling our little work, we propose to deal only with the facts of the present day, and living issues as they may present themselves.

It is well known that artificial incubation has been practiced, and attracted more or less attention for centuries, but it is only quite recently that it has been made practical.

That Incubators are now built that are thoroughly practical and combine merit and usefulness, no one will question, and it is our purpose to give a history, descriptive and comprehensive, of each of the leading machines now being offered to the attention of breeders. We shall also give attention to the care and management of the young chicks from the time they leave the shell until they are old enough to care for themselves, their diseases and little ailments and the simple remedies to use, striving to treat artificial Incubation from a thoroughly practical stand-point. With this brief preface we proceed at once to the subject in hand.

PRACTICAL ARTIFICIAL INCUBATION.

CHAPTER I.

ARTIFICIAL INCUBATION.

The many peculiar ideas that are expressed by various people regarding Incubation, by use of the various machines, are some of them ludicrous in the extreme. To any one who has stood by an incubator in some large exhibition and listened to the laughable remarks of the public, as they gaze upon the little lively balls of flesh and down, emerging from the broken shell, this fact will be appreciated. "How long does it take them to hatch out?" "Are they as good to eat as any others?" "Will they be healthy?" and hundreds of similar questions are heard on all sides. Prof. Brown in his recent work upon this subject remarks, "Many persons seem to think that Incubators work by magic, that they do the work in some swift and sudden manner, that is, the eggs are put in at the top, turn a handle and the chickens appear, or put the eggs in at night and they are hatched the

next morning, and seem to think it a waste of time
and energy if they do not hatch the eggs any quicker
than a hen." To a certain extent, an Incubator is a
very simple thing ; we well remember, when a boy, of
an old woman who made one, that worked quite successfully out of a dish-pan placed in a hole in the
seat of an old broken cane-seat chair. The pan being
filled with water an oil lamp was placed under it
to supply the heat, and the eggs were suspended in
a smaller pan in the water, each egg being wrapped
in soft cotton, and the whole covered with a warm
bed blanket. With *careful* watching success was
achieved. The woman had the several elements in
her crude machine which insure success. First, fertile
eggs ; second, an even, steady heat (secured in this
case by incessant watching) ; third, proper moisture,
and fourth (or you may place it first if you like), common sense. That an incubator is becoming a virtual
necessity to success and profit is becoming apparent.
You have a fine lot of fresh valuable eggs — no hens
can be found that are ready to undertake the task of
incubating them, boys are employed to scour the country around for " sitting hens," they are found, and readily you pay from six to twelve shillings apiece for each
hen, for your necessities are such that you must have
them. Now your trouble has begun—one hen changes

her mind after sitting steadily for a week, it is very cold weather, and the valuable eggs are wasted! Another quarrels with her neighbor; both finally sit upon the same nest; one nest is left to chill, the other nest nearly all broken with their quarreling—so it goes. Another hen is having a "splendid hatch," but she is a clumsy, club-footed bird, and one-half of the "pedigreed" chicks are dead in the shell on their natal day. Our readers will need no reminder of the troubles of the breeder in the "beautiful springtime." A practical machine is a necessity, and the question at once arises, which one shall I buy? There are but very few difficulties to be surmounted in using an incubator by persons possessed of a fair amount of common sense. The cardinal principle involved in them all is very similar. They save much trouble and vexation of spirit, but at the same time, we confess at once, that they, too, require a large amount of patience, and often many trials before success is finally achieved. There is a certain amount of "know how" that the successful user of an incubator must possess, which reminds us of the old story of the "gentleman of color" who was hired to dress a beaver-skin, and the job being accomplished in a very short time, the employer objected to the charge of three dollars, claiming that one dollar was surely enough, to which our sombre-hued friend replied, "Yes, Massa, one dollar for dressing the hide, and two dollars more for de know how."

The "know how" is a very necessary thing, yet at the same time we do not claim, that you must have the knowledge of a skilled mechanic, far from it, for many a boy or girl of twelve or fourteen years of age, or many a woman who, in addition to the cares of her small family, can run an incubator, and *successfully*, too. A great many people can be found who will denounce an incubator in strong terms, and our word for it, in a majority of cases, they are the very ones, who were the last to buy a mowing machine for their farms, a sewing machine for their wives, or a swinging cradle for their babies, and who always sternly set their face against every modern improvement, no matter what it may be, the march of civilization affects them both last and least of all.

Many things should be given due consideration before the purchase of an incubator is decided upon, and your mind must be fully made up upon a few points. 1st. Will you give it the attention and time that it will surely demand at your hands; and, 2d, will you persevere sufficiently in your efforts to gain success? This you must do, or better let it alone, and, not like a small boy with a scroll saw, throw it aside after one or two efforts, because you do not at once understand it, or break a few saw blades. No, you must use judgment tempered with moderation, and success will be your reward in this, as in any thing else.

You must give it time and attention, both during the process of incubation in its early stages, and more particularly so when the young chicks are emerging from their shells, and during their early stages of growth. There are a dozen little attentions required by the young chicks, many of which are usually provided by the mother hen. These they must have, and you will be compelled to give the necessary time for it. There is a trite saying, " If you wish a thing half done, send a boy, but if you wish it well done, do it yourself ; " this applies with great force to incubators, they cannot be left to everybody to care for ; you must give them your personal attention or that of a perfectly competent person, and indeed, if you are using several incubators, it will pay you well to employ a proper person to devote his entire time to their management. Another important adjunct is a place suitable to set up your incubator and run it ; it must be a place where the proper heat and temperature can be readily maintained. A great many breeders have a house built especially for their incubators, the same as they would build a house for their poultry, or more especially for their hatching-room and

young chicks. This room should be warm, properly
ventilated, but entirely free from drafts of air of
every kind. Now, dear reader, if you have decided
to give an incubator proper attention, and have a place.
prepared for its reception, the next thing to be decided will be, which one shall I buy? In order that
you may judge understandingly and come to a deci-
sion as to which may best meet your particular wants,
we shall give a thorough description of each machine,
and the particular points of excellence claimed for
each one by the respective manufacturers, and also
give the experience of prominent fanciers and breeders with various machines. You can then decide
intelligently, which you will prefer, for we are well
aware that what may meet one person's views may
be very far from another's, and an incubator well
adapted to one man's wants would be a failure in
the hands of some other person. Our descriptions
of both American and English machines will be
found to be very full and plain, illustrated properly,
and void of technique or usually incomprehensible
terms, and they are the result of two years' experience in examining the merits and demerits of the different machines. We commend each page to your
careful consideration.

CHAPTER II.

THE PERFECT HATCHER.

The inventor of the "Perfect Hatcher" says:
"In offering the Perfect Hatcher to the public, I do

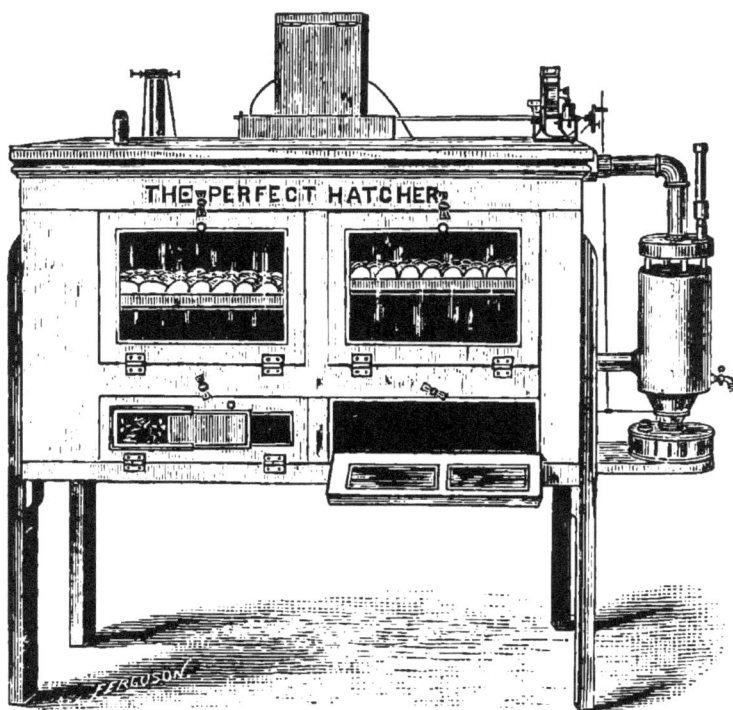

it under the firm conviction that I offer an article that
is properly named, as it has proved in my experience,
and that of all who have tried it, to be the most Per-

fect Incubator in all respects ever offered for sale. This opinion is given by parties that have used the best of other makers and found them imperfect in so many details as to make them only partially success- ful. I started out to establish a poultry farm on a large scale, to hatch broilers for the New York mar- ket, and I concluded that I could only make a success of it by hatching and raising artificially, as I thought that in no other way could I get out my chicks early enough to get the big prices.

" I was first attracted to the manure process but after a little investigation dropped that idea. I then pur- chased a very highly praised machine and commenced operations, filled it up with eggs and waited the result, which was a complete failure. I purchased another machine of another maker, that was a failure; pur- chased a third, and that was a failure, and I found the season ended, hundreds of dozens eggs destroyed, and not a dozen chicks left to tell the tale. I hatched in all, perhaps one hundred chicks, but they were so weak they all died but about a dozen which I raised up to three months and then they died too. But in all my experiments I had gained knowledge. I knew that chicks could be hatched if a proper incubator with all the necessary conditions for success could be devised, and I also discovered that of all the incubators that I had bought, not one of them possessed a single requisite of success. I concluded that I could build an incubator that could hatch chickens, and do it successfully, that I could combine the points necessary, viz., a perfect application of heat, a perfect ventilation, and perfect application of moisture applied automatically and continuous. I went to work and built my machine, and the principle then adopted proved I had hit exactly right, all that I needed was to develop and perfect it. This I have been at work for the past four years striving to accomplish, and I am happy to say have succeeded.

The application of heat in this incubator is by means of hot water in a galvanized iron tank which I claim to be the only correct method and nearest in imitation of nature. There are hot air machines, but I claim hot air is injurious to animal life as it is to plant life. You never see a green-house heated with hot air. It is always hot water. Neither do you see plants thrive in living rooms heated with a hot air furnace. The tank of this incubator is so arranged inside that the hot water when it first leaves the boiler is compelled to circulate around the outside edges and in all four corners of the tank while it is hottest, and through the center of the tank last, then downward through pipes at farthest end of the tank, then back to boiler by a gang of iron pipes located fourteen inches below the tank. By this means a perfect circulation of water is secured, and a perfectly uniform heat is established in every part of the machine, no one part being too hot and another part too cold, as is the case in all other hot water incubators, their makers not having been able to obtain a perfect circulation of water, without which a uniform and even heat cannot be obtained. You may heat water to the boiling point, and if it does not circulate it will not impart its heat, and the eggs will be cold when within two inches of the tank, but if a good circulation is secured the temperature of the water need be but a few degrees above that of the egg chamber.

"A perfect circulation of the water and application of the heat having been obtained, the next important step was to regulate the heat automatically, and so perfectly, that there would be no more variation than is had when the hen applies the heat. When she is on the nest, the heat of the eggs is kept perfectly uniform and I concluded this was a necessary condition to success, viz., to maintain a perfectly uniform, unvarying temperature, and to get a regulator that would accomplish this was the great problem. Mr. Edison had no greater struggle to perfect his light than I had to obtain this regulator. But after many weary trials I secured it, it is perfect and it is reliable. Every breath of cold or warm affects it, it is so exceedingly sensitive, and it acts at once; a twentieth part of a degree will change it. It acts very much quicker than mercury, and is unchanging in its qualities, never becoming inactive by use which mercury and all other forms of thermostats do. I found that electricity was the only agent that could be used in connection with this instrument, it was so very sensitive. By using electricity there is no friction to overcome, as there is when only a mechanism is used. When a mechanical contrivance alone is used the regulator or thermostat has to overcome the friction caused by the weight or spring that is used to operate the ventilators and the heat has to run up or down five or six degrees each way before the thermostat can pull the lever off the clutch to release the weight or spring. But in this incubator the regulator has to vary but the twentieth of a degree and it connects an electric circuit and acts on the electric magnet which releases the clock ma-machinery and the ventilators open and the lamps are turned down, thus effectually checking the heat. When the heat is checked the regulator vibrates again, closes another circuit, the ventilators close and lamps are turned up again, this operation goes on indefinitely and never fails to maintain a perfectly uniform

2

heat in the egg chamber. No matter how much it varies on the outside it will control the heat so perfectly that if the temperature drops to zero or rises to ninety the heat in the egg chamber will not vary, and I challenge the world to produce another machine that will do the same thing as well.

The adjustment of regulator to obtain any degree of heat desired is very simple and easily understood. It is done by two screws which are located upon top of machine in plain sight. To open the ventilators turn up screw No. 1 until it connects the circuit. To close the ventilators turn up screw No. 2 until it connects the opposite circuit. You can by this method adjust the regulator as fine as you can adjust a watch. You can set it so you can have one-twentieth degree variation or five to ten degrees as you desire. Now, in relation to the objection to the use of batteries, some of our rivals claim that none but an electrician or scientific person can use an incubator operated by electricity. This statement either shows their stupidity or their unfairness; there is nothing simpler than the use of the battery if directions are followed, and with our machine there is nothing that the purchaser needs to do with the battery only to just let it alone. There are no zincs to scrape once a week, no sulphate of copper to be put in every two weeks, or any thing of the sort.

When they leave our factory they are in condition to run for three years' constant use, and they are not to be touched by the owner. When they are finally exhausted we will supply new ones at low rates. The reason why these batteries last so long is that there is no perceptible consumption of them, for as before stated, we use two circuits, one to open and one to close the ventilators. The instant the circuit is completed and the wheels of the clock begin to move the circuit is again broken and the use of the electricity is only for a second. In all other incubators that use electricity to regulate with, the consumption of their batteries is very great for this reason, when the circuit is closed so as to open the ventilators the circuit remains closed until the ventilators close. In warm weather the ventilators will have to remain open ten minutes or over; during this time the battery is being consumed very fast, and ten minutes of a closed circuit will use up more of the battery than our machine will use in two months' constant use.

VENTILATION.

The ventilation is as perfect as any other part; the large air space in the egg chamber is a very important feature. The egg chamber is fourteen inches in depth, and below this chamber are the pipes and below the pipes is a second chamber, six inches in depth. This second chamber is fitted with doors same as egg chamber, in each door is a slide ventilator three inches wide by length proportioned to size of machine, four to ten inches. These ventilators are to be kept open all the time, either wide open or a little way, proportioned to the weather.

When the ventilators on top of the machine open to allow the hot air to escape, the cold air rushes in through all these ventilators, passes over the hot pipes and is warmed, and passes up into the egg chamber. This action occurs every twenty minutes, thereby keeping the eggs constantly supplied with fresh air; also the carbonic acid gas that is generated by the living chick in the shell, being heavier than common air, falls to the lower chamber below the pipes and is carried out by the cross currents of air that are in motion there through the bottom ventilators, and while the top ventilators are closed.

MOISTURE.

The moisture is applied automatically and continuously as in nature when the hen builds her nest on the ground, where the best results are always obtained. The ground is always moist, and the heat of the hen's body in addition to the heat of the sun is gradually and continuously drawing the moisture from the soil, the eggs receiving the benefit. Of course, eggs do not have to be sprinkled under these conditions. In our Hatcher the process is the same. We place galvanized iron pans on the hot water pipes beneath the egg tray and the water is warmed to just the right degree to evaporate fast enough to overcome the drying effect of the heat. The moisture from the pans is continuously rising, and is applied to the bottom of the eggs. The quantity of moisture can be increased or diminished as desired by the amount of surface of water exposed. To decrease the moisture we cover a portion of each pan ; to increase it, we remove the cover ; therefore, we have this part under perfect control, which is very important, as the egg, when fresh, is composed largely of water and a certain quantity must evaporate the first ten days of incubation ; if it does not, the eggs will addle. Thus it can be seen that if too much moisture is applied in the start we should fail to hatch any chicks, notwithstanding we had a perfectly uniform heat and ventilation. The application of moisture is of as much importance as either of the others. Thus it will be seen that a perfect hatcher must have all the conditions of success, such as named above, or failures will result oftener than successes, and that is why all the other machines in the market are partial failures, for not one of them has a suitable means for applying moisture; their eggs have to be sprinkled every day. It is true that some of them have pans of cold water underneath their egg trays, but cold water does not evaporate fast enough to supply the moisture, hence they have to sprinkle, and sprinkling the eggs at certain stages is too great a shock to the delicate germ.

TURNING THE EGGS.

As it is necessary to turn the eggs two or three times a day to make them germinate in a healthy manner, the labor of turning five hundred eggs, one at a time, is very great. It will take an hour to turn five hundred eggs, one at a time, and do it carefully. We furnish a simple method by which an entire drawer of one hundred eggs can be turned in ten seconds without touching the eggs with hands or jarring or disturbing them. No other machine furnishes such an arrangement.

THE EGG CHAMBER.

This possesses entirely new features, as before stated. It is fourteen inches in depth; which proves of great advantage in many ways. 1st. It gives an opportunity for a more equable diffusion of the heat through the chamber; it allows the eggs to be placed farther from the tank, and when the heat comes in contact with the eggs, it is softer and more genial than it would be if placed close to the iron tank, as in most incubators. 2d. We are enabled to adopt a plan by which we can have different degrees of heat, for instance in one drawer we can have 102°, a second 103°, a third 105°, etc. This is accomplished by having adjustable drawers. We can raise and lower our drawers a space of eight inches. The nearer to the tank a drawer is placed the higher the heat will be, say 105°. If we want 102° we lower the drawer far enough from the tank until 102° is obtained, or any other degree we desire. The drawers are adjusted in a moment by loosening the nuts and sliding the drawer where it is needed and tightening them again. This plan is of the greatest advantage, as it enables one to place eggs in at any time during incubation, which cannot be done in other machines for following reasons: When eggs have been in incubation eight days the circulation of blood in the chick begins to generate animal heat, and as a result the temperature of egg chamber begins gradually to rise, and a thermometer placed on the eggs will indicate about one degree higher than at first, by tenth day, and this heat of the eggs will continue to increase until the chicks die or the heat of chamber is decreased, or the egg drawer lowered from the heat.

"So it is obvious that eggs placed in the incubator with eggs that have been in ten days and placed on the same level with the latter cannot have the degree that is requisite, for eggs need the highest heat the first week (105°), and the lowest heat the last week (103°). Therefore, we place the drawer of fresh eggs at the highest position toward the tank, and those that are already in we lower a very little about every other day. Thus we are enabled to place eggs in every day if we desire, and give all their proper heat, and hatch with perfect success. This is a feature of great value, and possessed by no other machine. If we fill the machine full of eggs to start with, we simply reduce the heat of the whole apparatus after the eighth day by touching the regulating screws slightly every other day.

"The case is made of thoroughly seasoned wood, it is a double case with dead air space all around of one inch. Wood is the best non-conductor of heat and cold when it is combined, as we have it, with other non-conducting material. As before stated, our machine will stand a change in outside temperature of from 90° above zero down to zero and maintain a uniform heat. Some manufacturers lay great stress upon the iron case; I regard the iron case as a very poor affair. It is the best conductor of heat and cold in the world. I have seen their machines drop one degree of heat by simply opening the door and letting in a draft of air for an instant ; the fact is they fluctuate with the weather, and their makers say they must be placed in a room that will not get cooler than 50°, and that the temperature of the room must not vary more than ten to fifteen degrees. Besides they are not durable, they will rust out in two years and become valueless.

" The lower chamber of our Hatcher can be used as a nursery for a few days if desired. I have kept chicks there for six weeks.

PERFECT BROODER.

" Our Brooder is as perfect as our Hatcher, and the only one that can be used to advantage on a large scale. It is the only one that imitates the hen in brooding her chicks, viz., the chick presses its back close against the hen's body and is comforted by the warmth. In our Brooder, the chick presses its back close up against warm water pipes and is just as comfortable as when under the hen. In other brooders a tank is used and is placed eight or ten inches above the chicks; the chicks cannot come in contact with the heat which they crave doing; they consequently huddle together and on top of each other, and the result is, the weaker ones are always crushed, and you will find them dead every morning regularly until more than half the chicks are gone. In our Brooder we use 1 1-4 inch gas pipe covered with tarred paper and flannel, the pipes are within four inches of the floor; for very young chicks we put in a movable floor and bring them within two and a half inches of the pipes; as they increase in size we remove this extra floor. They never can get on top of each other, for there is not room enough, and they do not need to, as they are comfortable. The Brooder can be moved from place to place on the lawn and let the chicks run in and out at their pleasure. It can be closed up at night, and is a perfect protection against rats, cats and all other enemies; the chicks cannot get out until you let them out in the morning. The top is of glass with doors; so you can reach every part of it, and clean it out with ease. It is perfectly ventilated when closed up for the night.   The cost of oil to run it is not as great as the cost of the food for hens to raise the same number of chicks."

CHAPTER III.

THE RELIANCE INCUBATOR.

The inventor of the "Reliance" Incubator takes pleasure in offering to the public a machine which he believes to be the best yet invented for the purpose.

He claims:

First. "That it is more simple in construction than any of the popular Incubators now in the market.

Second. It is as positively automatic as any machine for the purpose yet invented.

Third. It is free from all electrical machinery and acids.

Fourth. It is more easily understood and managed more successfully than any other Incubator, and requires less attention, as ten minutes, twice in twenty-four hours (for a three-hundred egg machine) is amply sufficient, and it can be left to itself with perfect safety for the rest of the time, provided the instructions, which are very plain and simple, are obeyed.

Fifth. It costs less to run it, as it is necessary to heat but six quarts of water. (Other Incubators heat from eight to twenty gallons.)

Sixth. In the place of a tank of water, used in all other machines to heat the egg-drawer, I use a soap-stone radiator, placed over the egg-drawer, heated by an arrangement of hot water pipes, imbedded in the soapstone. In this manner I am able to heat the whole surface of the radiator all over alike, which has never yet been accomplished in any machine using a tank of water. Thus all parts of the egg-drawers are exactly the same temperature (obviating the necessity of changing the egg-drawers to keep all the eggs in the machine at the desired temperature).

Seventh. Perfect ventilation, and just the requisite amount of moisture.

Eighth. The machine is constructed entirely of metal and stone, therefore with proper care will last a life-time.

Ninth. Less liability to be affected by the outside temperature, as there is a dead air chamber over and around the entire machine.

Tenth. It will hatch all·the eggs that would hatch under the most favorable circumstances, in the natural way."

In the new departure he has instituted by inventing and using a soapstone radiator in preference to the tank of hot water, he has gained in several particulars, viz.: it is very much less sensitive to the changes of heat and cold, consequently in a large degree itself operates as a regulator to the temperature. He says, "I get a mild, soft heat, nearest like that developed from an animal body, in place of the sharp, burning heat, which every one will admit is developed from a metal tank of hot water; consequently it is better adapted to the purpose for which it is used, viz., the development of animal life.

The ventilation I claim to be perfect. Because (unlike any other machine) there is a ventilator over each egg-drawer (the egg-drawers are entirely separate from each other) that is never closed, and a plentiful supply of fresh air is constantly received into the bottom of the machine in such a manner that every corner of the nest is thoroughly ventilated all the time.

I do not open and close the ventilators for the regulation of the heat, but depend upon an entirely different device.

Evaporating pans are so constructed and placed as to give just the required amount of moisture to the eggs, and, at the same time, temper the air received into the machine, thus becoming an important auxiliary in regulating the temperature.

The eggs do not require sprinkling at any time. Instead of a common korosene lamp, such, as I believe, all other Incubator manufacturers use, I use a "Florence" oil stove (without doubt the best and most economical invention in which to burn kerosene oil for heating purposes), of a pattern made expressly for this machine, whereby I obtain a very much more even heat than can possibly be obtained from a common lamp, as well as very much more heat from the same amount of oil used, thus decreasing the expense of running.

In the use of soapstone I have furnished to the top of the eggs, heat that represents as nearly as possible that given off from the body of a hen or other fowl;

also a plentiful supply of cool air to the bottom of the egg-drawer, thus giving perfect ventilation, and cooling the eggs underneath with sufficient moisture, imitating nature as closely as it is possible for mechanical device to do.

There are, undoubtedly, two, and perhaps three Incubators now in the market, which are more or less successful, if sufficient time and attention are bestowed upon them; and I am fully prepared to sustain the assertion that notwithstanding they are supplied with thermostat or pyrometer they require more time and closer attention than the "Reliance," which makes use of neither. It was to dispense with the necessity for this extra close attention that automatic regulators of this class were invented and applied; but the important question is, do they accomplish the desired result? I claim they do not, and for the following reasons :

First. All machines with this description of regulator depend entirely on the working of the regulator for ventilation; consequently, should the flame of the lamp, by accident, be set so as to produce just heat enough to keep the egg-drawer at the desired temperature for several hours, the pyrometer or thermostat remains at rest, and the ventilator remains closed, and the air becomes foul (especially when it is near the time for the chick to leave the shell), which injures if it is not fatal to the incipient chick.

Second. A continuous irregularity of the heat in the egg-drawer is the unavoidable result of these regulators, because in order to have the regulator open the ventilator, the air in the egg-drawer must get too hot, and as it is of vital importance that the ventilator should open, it is necessary to purposely set the flame so as to produce too much heat, and after getting the egg-drawer too hot, the ventilator opens, and the machine gets too cool, when the ventilator is again shut, and immediately proceeds to get too hot again. And the three weeks' time is thus made up of fluctuating temperature, without a moment of even heat (unless by accident). And I claim that an even temperature with constant, perfect ventilation, is of vital importance to practical success.

Several of the most popular inventors and manufacturers of Incubators go so far as to state in their circulars that the ventilation of their respective machines is perfect, because the thermostat causes the ventilator to open every fifteen or twenty minutes, thus acknowledging that the temperature of the air in the egg-drawer is constantly and rapidly fluctuating.

"I claim that with even heat and constant, perfect ventilation, with sufficient moisture, a very much larger percentage of eggs will hatch and the chicks will leave the shell stronger and livelier than with uneven and fitful temperature and imperfect ventilation.

Again, the thermostat or pyrometer, by constant use for a few weeks, becomes, to a great degree, sensible to the change of the temperature, so that at least one of the manufacturers sends two pyrometers with each machine, with private instructions to change the same every twenty-four hours, in order to alleviate this difficulty.

This of course will be allowed to be an extra amount of labor ; and, as they generally have to be slightly altered each time, are a considerable care.

In conclusion, the machine in which the egg-drawer is most evenly heated, perfectly ventilated, and most easily managed, is worthy the attention of all desiring an Incubator — and such an one I believe the " Reliance " to be.

CHAPTER IV.

THE CENTENNIAL INCUBATOR.

Patented March, 1880.

This thoroughly practical machine has been before the public for a number of years; having received its

name from the fact of its first being exhibited at the
Centennial Exhibition, at Philadelphia, Pa., in 1876.

Since that time, however, it has been very much
altered and improved, being now constructed entirely
of galvanized iron and copper. All the heating parts
are of copper, encased and protected by galvanized
sheet iron ; the spaces between filled in with non-conducting material.   The body of the Incubator is
double — one case inside of the other — and the
intervening space is also filled in with a non-conductor.
This insures no waste of heat, and comparative protection from sudden changes in the outside temperature.

Lately, this non-conducting jacket has been doubled
in thickness, and improved material used for the filling,
so that the machine may now be used in a room where
water will freeze along side of it.   This improvement
has been added to specially fit it to the needs and
convenience of farmers and breeders who are not
fortunate enough to have a warm room or building
in which to run the machine.

Another advantage resulting from this construction,
is the durability of the Incubator.   In an investment
of this kind, the purchaser naturally does not wish to
incur a like expense every few years, and it is with
very much of the same feeling he would have in buy-

ing a watch : making a choice of one that will last him as long as he needs to use one. It has been conclusively proved that wood cannot be so thoroughly seasoned, but that it will be warped and twisted out of all shape, by the alternate agency of moisture and dryness, heat and cold. Hence, if encased in wood, the machine soon becomes defective and inoperative, the latter caused by the impossibility of keeping the regulating apparatus properly adjusted, every warpage and shrinking or swelling, throwing the parts out of place and entirely destroying their efficiency.

Since the adoption of the iron case, this is entirely remedied, and some machines which are now in use for the third season, are in as perfect working condition as when first sent out, never having had a repair or alteration put on them. Further, there is no reason to doubt but that the Incubator will remain in as good condition for ten or twenty years to come, if reasonable care is taken to draw off the water, dry it out and put it up when not in use.

Economy in running is another point to be considered in the purchase of a hatching apparatus ; and where it is intended to have one in use for any long period, the saving of oil will amount to quite an item. The smallest size of this make, — the No. 1 — with an actual capacity of one hundred and twenty eggs, will burn less than a pint of oil per day of twenty-four hours, and many have been run on a half pint per day. This (estimating the larger amount) with oil at present prices, will cost thirty-five cents to hatch one hundred and twenty eggs, or about one and one-third cents per day. The largest size " Centennial Incubator " —No. 4—holding over five hundred eggs, consumed, during the month of February, less than a quart daily. Allowing a full quart, the expense is about seventy-five cents to hatch five hundred eggs.

The entire freedom from smoke and bad smell is another, and a very pleasing feature of the machines of this make. This removes a serious objection to their being used in a dwelling-house.

But perhaps the strongest of the many good features of the " Centennial," is its simple and effective regulating apparatus. With no battery or electrical attachment, but a simple arrangement of levers, operated by a thermostatic bar, it is so perfectly self-regulating, that it may, and has been, left for two entire days, during which the extreme variation, as shown by a self-registering thermometer, was but two and one-half degrees.

It is this quality of perfect self-regulation, so simple that children can, and do operate the machine, that has given it such a popular hold among the fanciers of the country. And, although higher in price than many other makes, it is in more general use, and giving the best of satisfaction.

Our fanciers, as a class, are rather slow to adopt incubators, or any other mechanical device pertaining to their special pursuit ; but the " Centennial " seems to have won its way very quickly, yet surely, into the good opinion and confidence of the leading men in the fraternity. The indorsement of such well-known fanciers as P. Williams, Jas. M. Lambing, Geo. S. Josselyn, W. H. Todd, Jno. J. Berry, E. R. Spaulding, D. D. Bishop, C. A. Keefer, and a host of others, would seem to indicate that incubators and artificial incubation have reached a very high degree of perfection in this particular machine.

A strong point, and one which has contributed not a little to its success, is the exceptionally large percentage of chickens hatched. Whether in experienced hands, or under the care of a novice, the result almost invariably exceeds the average natural process. From whatever cause, whether the uniform heat in all parts of the egg-drawer, or the system of thorough ventilation, or the peculiar construction of the egg-chamber, giving the top of the eggs a warm, dry atmosphere, and the bottom a cool, moist one, or the method of turning the eggs, or all combined,

there is certainly less loss of eggs, and a smaller percentage of weakly chickens, than with any other
apparatus now in use.

In the brooding of the chicks, the CENTENNIAL BROOD-
ER stands at the head of the list. Subjected, as it has
been, to the severest tests, it has proved to be the only
one which can be used in the open air in all weathers,
and perfectly shelter and protect the chicks from cold
and wet, as well as from rats, minks and other prowl-
ing vermin.

The heating arrangement is composed of a thin galvanized iron tank, fed by a small boiler, which is heated
by a small kerosene lamp. This tank is so placed, that
the chicks of different ages and sizes may all receive
equal benefit from it; and it is also sheltered from the
outer air by a galvanized iron roof, or cover. The front
half of the brooder is covered with glass, making a
warm dry run for the chicks, in cold or wet weather.
The lamp of the size for eighty chicks, holds one-half
pint of oil, which will burn from two to three days.
Several sizes are made, accommodating from twenty
up to one hundred chicks. Many prominent fanciers
are using from two to half a dozen of the brooders,
having discarded hens entirely for the taking care of
the chicks; and it seems to be the universal opinion
of those who have thoroughly tried them, that fully

twenty per cent more chicks can be raised by means of the brooders, than with hens, and that the chicks are larger and more healthy.

One more essential aid to the artificial process, is the egg tester; with it the non-fertile eggs can be detected by the third or fourth day after being under heat: removing them gives room for other and fertile eggs, and thus saves space and time. At a still later or more progressed state of incubation, those which have started and died can be discerned and removed, avoiding unpleasant smells in the egg drawer.

H. W. AXFORD,

INVENTOR AND MANUFACTURER OF THE NATIONAL INCUBATOR

CHAPTER V.

THE NATIONAL INCUBATOR.

The "National" is more commonly known as the "Axford," being manufactured by H. W. Axford & Co.. at Chicago. Probably no incubator has achieved

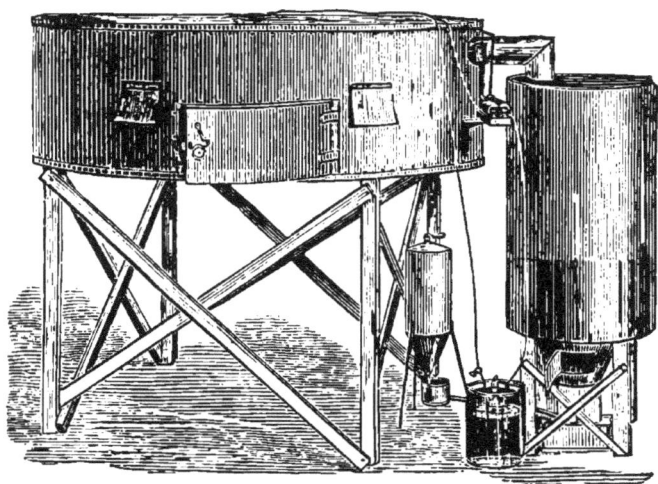

such large results, as it has been exhibited a great deal.

"A review of what a thing has done is the best proof of its merits. It was invented in 1874, and ever since the brothers have given their whole time to perfecting the machine, studying the egg and the necessary care to hatch out the chicks. Their first exhibit was made at the Great National, Chicago, in the winter of 1875, then Detroit, Omaha, St. Louis; from thence they made a remarkable trip of two or three days on board the steamer J. L. Rhodes, to Louisville. The incubator was set up on the forward cabin deck, and hatched chicks all the way on the river, much to the astonishment of the passengers. At night it was surrounded by some canvas to protect it from the wind. Then it was successfully exhibited at Cincinnati, Harvest Home, Pittsburgh, Allegheny Exposition, "Second National," Chicago, Indianapolis, Chicago, 1876, Indianapolis, second year, Chicago, 1877, "Third National," Chicago, Fort Wayne (Ind.) Fair, Toledo (Ohio) Fair, Fat Stock Show, Chicago, Terre Haute, Ind., and the "Great International," Buffalo, N. Y., 1879. Then at the Grand exhibit at Toronto, visited by 35,000 persons, Fat Stock, Chicago, 1879, the Great National at Indianapolis, 1880; Springfield and Worcester, Mass. From the great variety of these exhibits, hatching by the hundreds and thousands, we must conclude it a decided success—pleasing the public. In the spring of 1879, with eggs raised on their own place, one hundred and seventy-nine chicks were hatched from one

hundred and eighty eggs in the smallest size incubator. This must not be considered so very wonderful,
for it must be borne in mind that all infertile and un-
sound eggs are discarded, and there is no reason why
in a successful incubator every egg should not bring
forth a chicken.

They have shown beyond a doubt, chicks can
be raised by artificial means, never sparing of proof,
selling from their Toronto exhibit three thousand
chicks alone ; at Springfield, Mass., twelve hundred,
and the demand was so great that many more were
needed, as the officers of the society can testify. The
fifty chicks brought from the Indianapolis show to
Springfield, which were then two weeks old, were
quickly bought up.

The machine has been constructed so as to comply
with all the laws of nature, and the demands of the
chicks — supplying them with fresh air, sufficient
moisture, and uniform heat. The only work seems to
be in turning the eggs, which must be done in order
to get perfect chicks.

It is very easy to turn seven hundred in twenty
minutes. The work of heating and regulating will
not be fifty minutes for a hatch. No patented ventilating pipes are needed to carry cold air to the bottom of the eggs, which, at the same time, is supposed

to take off the carbonic acid gas from the eggs, but
simply a few holes punched through the bottom,
through which the cold air and heavy gases fall of
their own specific gravity. Turning devices (are
claimed by them) to the present time as useless, as
quite a large percentage of the eggs are not turned,
and some are killed all through the process, except in
large ovens containing only a few eggs—but here—
costing more than they are worth to hatch. Eggs
are easily tested, and with the peculiar make of
their "egg tester," the *chick's heart* may be seen to
beat in forty-eight hours after being set. This is an
important feature, as those eggs having no chicks may
be used in the house. While with the tester commonly sold, it requires from seven to eight days to see
the development, but by this time the eggs are ruined.

Mr. Axford claims for his incubator that it is practical to run it in any temperature, and that you do not
have to "regulate the room," and that the great principle of the incubator lies in its construction, which
admits the heat to the egg oven only as the temperature falls, and when the desired degree has been
reached the heat is shut out and retained in the
heater for future use, thus increasing its heating
power, enabling it to sustain a proper amount of heat
on the eggs throughout the widest range of temper-

ature; were this not the case, it would send all the heat the lamp produces into the oven, and then allow the surplus to escape, admitting cold air into the egg oven, causing a local low temperature among the eggs, and destroying a large percentage of chicks.

The Messrs. Axford have given twenty-nine public exhibitions of their incubator in successful operation, and over two hundred thousand people have seen it, and witnessed to its wonderful success, and through the medium of these exhibitions their incubator has attained a national popularity.

It is just and right that gentlemen who give so much attention to the subject as have the Messrs. Axford, should be amply rewarded with success. It is a subject that a very large class are interested in, and they should thank those inventors who struggle through years of adversity to perfect inventions that are a great public benefaction. The incubator is daily growing in popularity, and it will not be long before they will be used by nine-tenths of the successful breeders.

If we could have a tournament upon a grand scale, in which all the various incubator manufacturers would take part, we think it would do a great deal to make them more sought after.

We believe the Messrs. Axford are desirous for a

friendly contest of this kind the present year, and we hope the other manufacturers will respond favorably.

CHAPTER VI.

THE SMITH INCUBATOR.

In a letter to our editor, Mr. F. M. Smith, of Syracuse, thus speaks of his incubator :

" I began with the notion that an egg immersed in an atmosphere of suitable temperature and humidity, would advance through successive stages of embryonic development, till the perfectly formed chick emerged in due time from the shell. I constructed several forms of *hot air machines*, but found that while the temperature was easily controlled, the question of *moisture* was involved in much difficulty and uncertainty, and finally to secure a solid basis of *fact* for the regulation of this important condition, I weighed the eggs under sitting hens, at intervals of three days through the period of incubation ; I learned by this means that the loss of weight under natural conditions was uniform and amounted to about one-sixth or sixteen per cent average from the time of sitting to the hour of pipping the shell. After a sufficient ex-

4

perience with the hot air principle I concluded I was
on the wrong track, and adopted the top-heat system.

A water-tank heated by kerosene lamps and suspended over the eggs furnishes, by downward radiation, the heat for incubation in my machines as now
constructed.

A second and independent tank heated by an independent lamp, suspended beneath the entire egg
chamber, furnishes also the bottom heat, although the
" heat " from this source does not amount to much.
The office of the lower or " moisture lamp " is to impart a proper and uniform humidity and temperature
to the incoming air currents, and easily obviates all
the difficulties encountered in the hot air plan. Both
tanks are made of large capacity, ten to twenty gallons
or more, so that changes of temperature are very slow,
and should the lamps go out entirely, no sensible
change is observed in the temperature of the eggs for
a period of twelve hours or more. The upper tank
especially is well encased in non-conducting material,
and comparatively independent of external influences.

The peculiar and distinguishing feature of my incubator — so far as I am aware — is the construction of
the heating tank, by means of which the incoming air
currents, after first passing over the surface of the
water in the moisture tank, becoming properly modi-

fied in temperature and humidity, and thence passing through the egg tray, cooling and ventilating the eggs, finally pass into the upper or heating tank and over the surface of the hot water contained in it, and thence out through the ventilator.

This arrangement furnishes an instant and powerful means of regulating and checking any excess of temperature through the large evaporation thus effected in the upper tank, as may be readily understood by any one familiar with the dynamics of heat and evaporation. It renders the incubator comparatively independent of the heat of summer days, or the chilly air of other seasons, although, for many reasons, it is always desirable to operate an incubator in an air of mild and uniform temperature—60° to 80°, say.

The loss of water thus effected must be carefully and periodically replenished—once a week usually—pure soft water being requisite, entirely free from any sediment or saline contents.

The power for opening the ventilator is supplied by a galvanic battery of two cells usually, which at the same time furnishes the most delicate and sensitive means of regulating the temperature, through the operation of the pyrometer or thermostatic bar, which constitute a part of the galvanic circuit.

This pyrometer of very simple construction is easily sensitive to one-twentieth of one degree, Fahr., and serves to keep the heating tank at an almost perfectly uniform temperature. The ventilator, which is operated directly from the armature of an electro-magnet, will open and close several times per minute, while no change whatever can be detected in a thermometer placed alongside the pyrometer and similarly exposed. The ventilator thus opens and cools eggs, tanks, and all, whenever the temperature reaches the maximum point fixed by the regulating screw. A slight fall in temperature again closes the ventilator. There is no other machinery whatever connected with my incubator—no clock-work, wheels, levers, circulating pipes—or other device to suffer derangement by use or accident. It is believed to be as simple as it is possible to construct any machine which can safely and reliably conduct so delicate and wonderful an operation as the *incubation of an egg*, the epitome of all animal life.

Another feature of my incubator, which is unusual, is a small artificial mother or brooder, and pen, occupying the entire top, into which the little chicks are introduced soon after being hatched, and where they are confined for the first few days after life, or until they learn to eat and drink well and get fairly " on their legs." I have found this an extremely useful and convenient arrangement. The brooder is warmed by the waste heat from the machine, is continuously ventilated with warm air, and in it the little chicks lie about, not huddled and packed together, but scattered apart in entire comfort. Many interesting details might be added with reference to the management of the incubator—the selection, testing, and development of the eggs, etc., but which do not appear to come within the scope of this article.

As to proportion of eggs which can be hatched it is difficult to affirm any thing very definite, so much depends upon the attentiveness and judgment of the operator, and also upon the character of the eggs used.

Some eggs appear to be endowed with very vigorous vitality and will stand much abuse; others are feebly endowed and require the most careful management, and often fail with that. In general, with fair management, and no protracted over-heating, a hatch of sixty to eighty per cent of the fertile eggs may be expected. With exceptionally good eggs a larger percentage can be realized, and with exceptionally poor ones, the result is proportionately reduced.

The cost of operating is about six to eight cents per day for kerosene and battery power.

I usually make two sizes, viz., of two hundred and three hundred egg capacity—selling respectively for $55 and $65. Incubators can be made of any size and capacity to order at corresponding prices, although I have found a machine above three hundred capacity to be an unwieldy article of furniture.

The eggs require turning at least twice daily, especially during the first ten days of incubation, and during the second ten days should be removed from the machine at least every other day and cooled down to 80° or 75° — during half or three-quarters of an hour. A little longer does no harm. I was very skeptical about this practice until a few accidental exposures of this sort convinced me of its necessity and utility. As to the time required, about half an hour to an hour daily is sufficient for all necessities. The eggs require a periodical testing — the unfertile and dead ones being removed.

The thermometers are placed in direct contact with the eggs, on top—thus constantly disclosing the actual temperature of the *eggs themselves.*

My incubator has taken the first premium for two successive years at the exhibitions of the Empire State Poultry Association in this city, 1879–1880; also at the Onondaga County Fair, in the fall of 1879. With the exception of one contract exhibition at Cortland this winter, these are the only public exhibitions I have made. At one exhibition this winter I hatched about three hundred chicks from five hundred eggs set. As I explained to you in my former letter, it is only somewhat recently that my incubator has been perfected, and afforded results that have established my confidence in its utility and novelty — as well as settled my purpose to offer it to the poultry dealing world in competition with the incubators of other make."

CHAPTER VII.

THE ECLIPSE INCUBATOR.

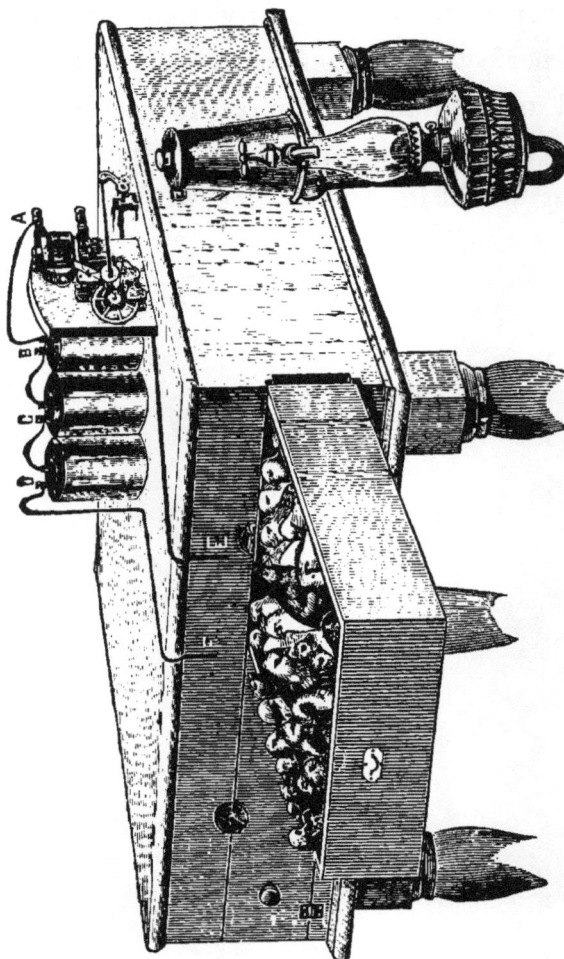

"That poultry husbandry has become one of the largest of our productive industries is now quite generally appreciated and admitted," and in whatever branch of the business in which one may be engaged, the artificial process of incubation shows at once its manifest advantages over the slow and uncertain natural process. Do you raise fancy stock or high-class poultry for exhibition? Observe what birds are bearing off the prizes; the chances are ten to one that they were hatched artificially, and this will appear obvious enough when we consider that, being hatched *early*, they get through with their moulting early, and show their superiority at the exhibitions, during the fall and winter, by being more fully matured.

If broilers are wanted for the early market, how can they be supplied in quantity unless they are hatched artificially? Biddy is altogether too uncertain to depend upon for these very toothsome articles of food, even if she feels inclined to begin the task, when her services in this line are most in demand; and should she be accommodating enough to begin, the probability is that you will sooner or later have to be there too to hold her down, or lose the eggs. We know to our sorrow that Biddy will often cackle when she ought to cluck. In fact, you might just as well expect a train of cars to travel without a locomotive as to expect to raise broilers without an incubator.

If you make a specialty of raising eggs for the market, you will find the incubator invaluable, for the best layers are unquestionably the non-setters. When artificial incubation becomes universal here, as it must in time, probably all the breeds will in a great measure lose the desire to set; it is the case in some parts of Europe, and why not here? If we can hatch and raise chickens better without hens than with them, the sooner they surrender to us the better; they can serve us much better by producing the eggs, which we *at present* cannot do.

There are manufactured for sale to-day some thirty or more incubators, many of which are comparatively worthless, some of them fraudulently so. Every manufacturer claims his particular machine to contain *all* the essentials and conveniences for successful incubation, and that his particular machine is the only one that does contain them. Now, when a person wishes to purchase an incubator, he naturally wants one that will surely meet its requirements; so we suggest to the reader the following: Having made up your mind that you *need* an incubator, and that you understand what is necessary in order to be successful, send for circulars to as many of the different manufacturers as you may hear of, and, having obtained them, compare them carefully; satisfy yourself as to whether their contents is the truth or not, and the one you then like the best is the one with which you will in all probability meet with the most success. But beware of all *secrets* about an incubator. Before you send your money you have a right to know the why and wherefore of every part and point of the incubator, and if the maker cannot satisfy you on the point it will evidently not bear investigating. Again, beware of a manufacturer who fills up his circulars with accounts of failures of other incubators; it is not an honorable way of doing business, and an honorable man would never do it. The accounts may be true in part; for there is not an incubator made, and never will be, but what has failed in some hands; but when he cannot make a sale without doing this, his incubator is one which will never commend itself.

New incubators are starting up every day, which are destined to "astonish the world," but their careers are of short duration. Sooner or later most of those now made must drop from the list, as there is not sale enough to support so many. There is room in this country for four or five, but not more. The best of those now manufactured will stand by their own recommendations, and be improved from time to time as necessity dictates. The manufacturers should give their incubators their undivided attention, in order to secure the best results.

That there have been total failures with every incubator made is apparent enough, but it should not *always* be laid to the incubator Much depends upon the eggs, their age, fertility, etc., and upon local circumstances; and there are some things about which little is known yet for a certainty. Much jarring has always been considered fatal to the eggs, and also a long chill. But last summer I took one of our Eclipse incubators in an express wagon twice across the city of San Francisco, Cal., then put it aboard of a freight train for Sacramento, distance 150 miles. It went in the caboose at the end of the train, the door of which was so narrow that the incubator had to be put on its side, in order to get it in, and was taken out in the same way; of course all the eggs were rolled about, and for *twenty-six hours they were stone cold.* The jerking and banging of the train was tremendous, yet, strange as it may appear, almost every egg in the machine hatched, and most of them on time. Some of the eggs were due the day the journey was finished, the others every day during a week. This was at the California State Agricultural Fair, and the incubator *took the society's medal.* As the same thing has happened since, under almost the same circumstances, it would seem to show that eggs under incubation can endure some pretty rough handling.

It is to be hoped that this book, which is something entirely new, will be found to contain much valuable information for those interested in the subject. In the United States, artificial incubation is not generally well understood at present: but one thing is certain, which is, that *here* is where it will be brought to perfection. The writer has been in nearly every country on the western continent, from British America to Cape Horn, along both oceans and in the interior, all over the West Indies, and a little on the other side of the Atlantic. Everywhere the great benefits of poultry are well known, and in many places nothing can be more profitable than poultry husbandry.

The labor required to manipulate an incubator is very light, and a woman can do it just as well, if not much better than a man. The successful machines all regulate themselves, or ought to; so they require but little time, and this little in the morning and evening, when it can be best spared.

The manufacture of the Eclipse is now our sole business. We have a large, roomy shop, furnished with steam power, containing seven rooms, with every facility and convenience for carrying on the business as it should be done.　We make every effort to have the machines first class in every respect, and honestly believe there is no more practical or convenient incubator in existence.　They are economical in consumption of fuel, thoroughly and completely ventilated, well built and elegantly finished.　Our circulars containing a complete description of the incubator, will be sent to any address upon application."

CHAPTER VIII.

THE CORBETT APPARATUS.

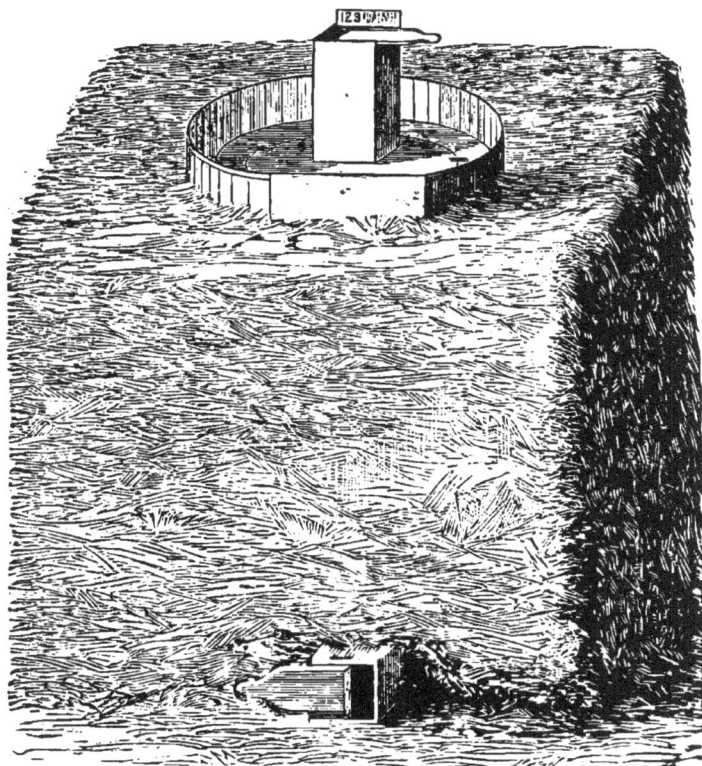

This incubator is the invention of Prof. A. Corbett, of New York, who has followed in the footsteps of the celebrated Reaumur, who was a member of the Academy of Sciences in Paris in 1747. After several years of experience, Prof. Corbett is assured that he has made the process practicable, and a patent was duly issued to him June 27, 1875. Our first illustration represents the apparatus in operation, surrounded by manure, and containing the eggs in process of incubation ; the second illustration shows the inside of the machine, and the third shows it transformed into an artificial mother. Upon this apparatus Prof. Corbett has received forty-five medals and diplomas, including those of the Centennial Exhibition, the Chili Exposition, and leading agricultural fairs. He has about $75,000 invested in the poultry business; and a work entitled "The Poultry Yard and Market," of which he is the author, has gained for him considerable notoriety. In this work, from a chapter entitled "Researches and Success," we extract the following :

RESEARCHES AND SUCCESS.

" The public will now understand from what sources I have sought to learn ; and after all the experiments I have made, I concluded at last that Reaumur's system appeared to be most feasible, it being the easiest and least expensive to follow. I therefore from that time began to practice it, thus: Six casks were placed in a heap of manure, and 600 eggs were placed in

them. All were lost. It was in winter, and I thought

5

that in the cellar the casks would keep at a better degree of heat; but there not being room enough, and the want of ventilation, were the causes of my failing. Not in the least discouraged, although disappointed, I again placed eight casks under an old shed, and this time put 800 eggs in them; the success would have been entire, had not the rain fallen one day on part of the manure heap, and cooled it off. Nevertheless, from the other part I proved the success, and you can judge how delighted I was to see several hundred young chickens hatched.

Let the reader rightly understand that we did not have entire confidence in the success to be derived from this venture at the time, as it was necessary to find a place to put the newly-hatched chickens in, which appeared to us like a true army of invaders. Those persons who have never seen hundreds of young chickens of one and two days old, can form no idea of the busy and noisy household. Luckily, we had an artificial mother, warmed by one lamp, and I placed the young chickens in it; whether it was the smell of the kerosene that was injurious to them, or whether the heat produced by the hot water did not accomplish the wished-for object, I lost the greater number of them, and I had the misfortune to prove that it was especially from crowding themselves in the corners that they died. This was a bitter disapуoint-

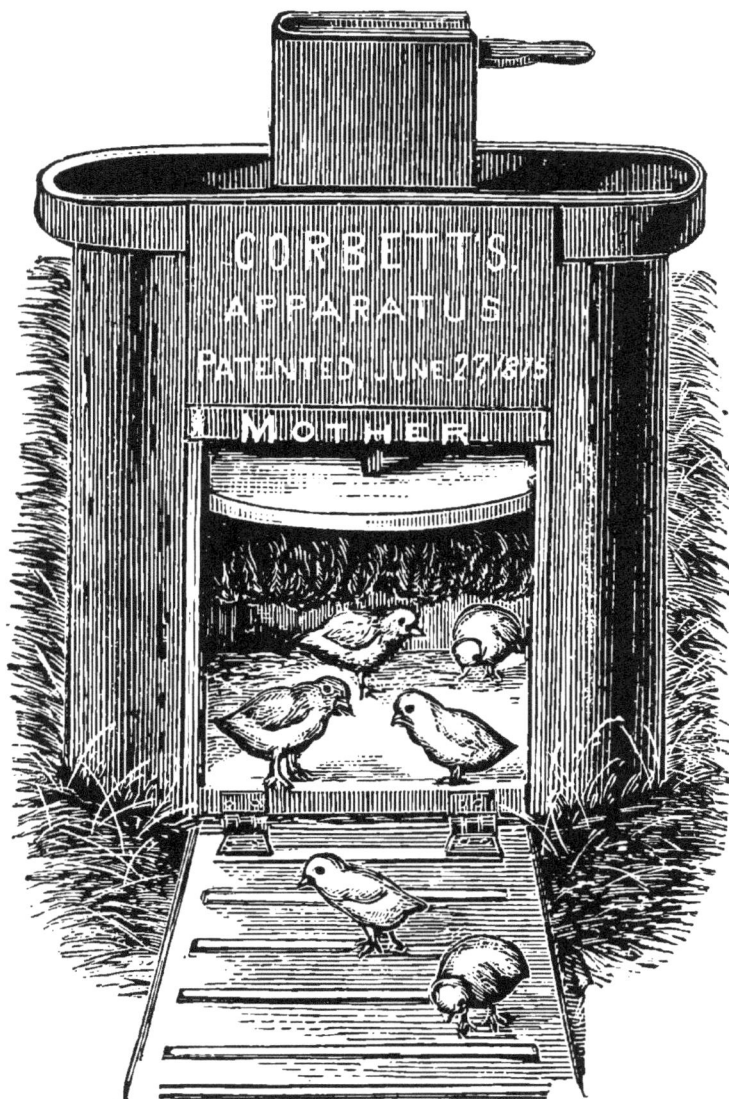

ment to me. As there was now no doubt that I could

hatch the eggs with the aid of manure, it only re-
mained to improve on the casks and mothers, and the
manner of directing or regulating the heat, besides
providing the proper and necessary ventilation, and to
supply the necessary quantity of air.   I, first of all,
began my improvements on the artificial mother, in
suppressing the corners as much as possible, and at
last had one built without corners, measuring twelve
feet in length and ten feet in width, and warmed by
two kerosene stoves.   I thought myself very happy in
having such a large artificial mother, in which I could
place 1,800 chickens of different ages.   Every thing
was complete in it — park, perches and ventilation.
Unfortunately, one night in April one of the lamps
exploded and set on fire the building which it was in,
and which measured 200 feet in length and cost $6,000.
The dog gave the alarm, and soon every one on the
farm was awakened, and commenced to extinguish the
fire by means of the India-rubber hose kept on the prem-
ises for such a calamity, and with a plentiful supply of
water the building was saved by a miracle, but I was
not so fortunate with my young brood; nearly all of
them were smothered or suffocated.   Again was I
forced to resign myself to fate and give up the raising
of my pullets artificially by means of lamps.   The
insurance company paid the damage to the building,
but the poultry was not insured.

Having got over this loss, I puzzled my brains to find a new system, and began to think I should have to renounce the idea, when the happy thought struck me to try the manure heap, and to see if I could not make it do for the chickens what it did so well for the eggs. I then placed a common box in the manure and put in it some newly hatched chicks; this was rather a bold proceeding, for the chances were that I should only find dead ones in the morn-ing. Judge of my surprise when at five o'clock in the morning I opened the box and saw all these little ones with their large eyes open, waiting their first meal, and they were quickly fed.

This, then, was the solution of the great problem. Was it chance or luck? Nevertheless, I had before me the fact that there were animated beings born in manure and receiving the warmth necessary for their welfare from the same source. Having already received so many checks and deceptions, I hesitated and re-frained from shouting "Victory!" — Eureka it might be.

A few more days would show me what success I might depend on in using this means of raising them, and all those that were daily hatched received the same treatment. At length, after fifteen days' experience, I had only to fight against the corners of the box; for

those who have the opportunity of visiting an establishment for rearing young chickens know full well
how they will crowd into the corners; the stronger
ones mount on the backs of the weaker, and these are,
almost in all cases, victims to their companions.

I now began to look for a box that would in a certain degree resemble the hen. Everybody knows that
if she gives warmth to the chickens it is by covering
them with her wings; but again, if an account was
taken of the number she crushes by treading on them,
of those she loses in walking round with them, you
can easily see that the raiser pays dearly for the heat
she gives. I will admit there are some mothers pat-
terns of gentleness, tenderness and carefulness, and
quite worthy of the praise and admiration bestowed
on them, and will allow several authors to say all they
can in their favor; but if they were, like myself, daily
watching them, and convinced of the reality, they
would soon see how very many in general destroy
their young; it is by millions yearly that they could
be counted. Up to the present time very few have
troubled themselves about this great question, for the
simple reason that this enormous loss, being shared by
all, it has not awakened the attention of the great
poultry raisers. One of my neighbors, who raises a
great quantity of poultry, especially turkeys, lost in

one day sixty-four chicks, their careful mothers having taken them off to a distance, when the rain came and they were lost. This man, a clever farmer, suffering so great a loss, has he ever thought he might avoid it? I don't believe he has.

In order that my apparatus should be good, I kept strict account of the heat given to the chickens by the mother, the movement of the wings, and especially of the amount of air that penetrated under her. After several days' labor and combinations, I succeeded in obtaining all these results, and I found I had replaced the hen with great advantage, for really my apparatus is much superior to the hen. The stomach and the wings are, by a clever combination, beautifully imitated. Especially do chickens find this to be the case whilst growing up as well as when they are small. This apparatus having so admirably succeeded in raising chickens, why could it not serve also to hatch them? To this important question I could not immediately reply; so I began another experiment, and the first trial failed, and upon my making further researches I discovered that what prevented the success of the incubation was simply in the quality of the wood of which the boxes were made. I then made another apparatus and new experiments, and at last succeeded.

From that day I found I had solved an important problem, and that I could hatch and raise chickens without the assistance of any lamp, nor with any fire, and that manure alone would do it. Ah! if Reaumur could rise from his ashes, how happy would he be to see these facts established; and I would wish to see present near the hatching broods those authors who have so little gratitude for this renowned man of the past century."

"Every pen that is employed in the praise of any subject or industry does honor to the author who renders justice to the merits of others, more especially when it alludes only to their memory."

CHAPTER IX.

SUCCESSFUL ENGLISH INCUBATORS.

Artificial incubation has made fully as much progress in England the past two years as in America. In 1877 it began to attract the attention of the practical, progressive breeders in that country, and has been steadily gaining in favor with them ever since. It has been largely encouraged by frequent trials of the different machines at public exhibitions or " Incubator Tournaments," as they are called, in which the various machines are put to the test under similar circumstances, and these public trials attract great attention.

The one held at Hemel Hempstead last year was very noteworthy in many respects, the best, or most successful machine hatching, 97 per cent, the second one 57 per cent, the third 56 per cent, the fourth 43 per cent, and several others were nearly as successful. The trial took place in the month of September, and we can all understand that there are many adverse circumstances connected with a trial of that kind, and that time of the year, which should be given due consideration.   For the descriptive part of the English machines, we are indebted to a recent work upon this subject by the editor of the Fanciers' Chronicle (English.)

CELEBRATED ENGLISH INCUBATORS.

CHRISTY'S HYDRO-INCUBATOR.

This machine is the invention of Mr. Thomas Christy, London, and we believe, so far as the mode of working is concerned, he obtained his idea from the Rouillier incubator used so much in France; he has made several alterations, which he considers improvements, but as we have not yet had an opportunity of testing the Rouillier, we cannot express an opinion upon them.   The Christy machine is about 30 inches square, and outwardly has an appearance of a wood chest with a drawer at the bottom and a glass gauge above; in fact, it has very little appearance of being an incubator from its outward aspect, having none of the mechanical contrivances that are generally to be seen on these machines.   It is simply a tank occupying two-thirds of the whole, the remaining third being taken up with the egg drawer.   This tank has some internal compartments which divide the water, the objects of which will shortly be seen.   The inlet to the tank is on the top, and the outlets, of which there are two, are at the

front.   One of these is about half-way down, the other
being fixed at the bottom of the tank.   The gauge
glass, of course, registers the height of the water in
the tank.   A wooden door, on being removed, reveals
the egg drawer, which, on being drawn out, shows the

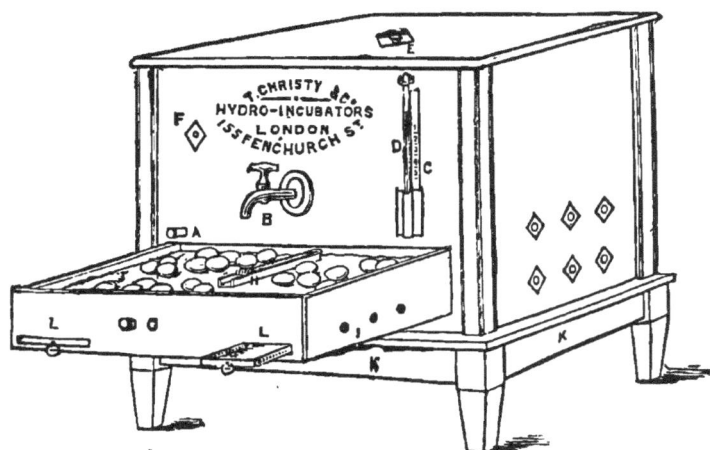

HYDRO-INCUBATOR FOR 100 EGGS.

A is the pipe only used for completely emptying the cistern ; B, the brass tap for
drawing off the water prior to replenishing the cistern with boiling water ; C, the
glass gauge with a marked scale, D, at the side to register height of water in the cistern ; E, the pipe for filling the cistern ; F, the tube for escape of air when water is
put in the cistern ; G, the drawer into the front of which the new earth-trays slide ;
H, thermometer in the drawer ; I, I, the air-holes in sides of incubator and drawer ;
J, the flannel ; K, the stand or box used to keep the incubator off the ground ; L, the
earth-trays.

thermometer, and   the arrangements for moisture.
The eggs are placed upon a perforated zinc tray, the
holes allowing the moisture to rise from the earth
trays beneath, and keeping the bottom of the eggs
cool.   Air is admitted by two rows of holes at each

side of the machine, one row of which admits air into the drawer above the eggs, and the other below the eggs.

The marvelous part of the whole thing is, that it works without lamps or gas, and, therefore, needs no regulator, which is always the most expensive and difficult part of a self-regulating incubator. The mode of procedure is to fill the machine with boiling water, which raises the heat up to about 120 or 130 degs., and after allowing it to cool down to 102 degs., keep the heat at about that temperature by drawing off every twelve hours, by the tap placed midway in the tank, a sufficient quantity of water, and replacing it by the same quantity of boiling water. Strange though this may seem, if it is properly done it will keep the temperature pretty even. The quantity requiring to be taken out varies with the outer temperature, and whilst a very small quantity of water will work it in summer, or if kept in a warm room in winter, if kept in a cold place it takes a large quantity to keep it going.

This machine, as will have been apparent to our readers, can only be worked where a sufficient supply of hot water can be obtained. In summer, or if kept in a warm place, this can be done quite easily, but in the depth of winter — the time when Incubators are

of the most use — the difficulty is not so easy to overcome.　Of course, a large pan can be got to hold three
or four gallons of water, but it is not every household
that can allow the fire to be monopolized for an hour
or two twice a day.　In large establishments, where
the kitchen boiler is always pretty near boiling point,
the thing is easily managed, but the majority of those

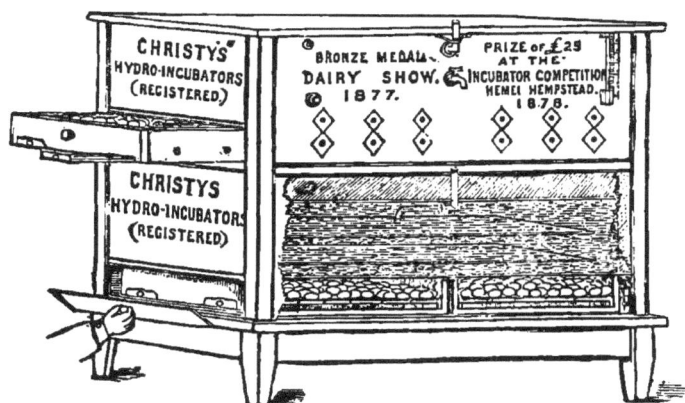

HYDRO-INCUBATOR FOR 500 EGGS.
Constructed with two cisterns and four drawers, each cistern working independently
of the other.

who have incubators have not this convenience.　Our
own plan was as follows : — We placed the incubator
in a dressing-room adjoining the bath-room, and upon
the top of the incubator put a small gas stove, upon
which a large tin boiler, holding about seven gallons
of water, was placed.　As the heat of the water in
the bath boiler was generally from 150° to 180°, it did

not require a great deal of time to boil it ; and, a tap being fixed in this tin boiler right above the inlet pipe, the water, *actually boiling*, was run into the machine. It is necessary, when this is done, to place a sheet of tin under the gas stove, or the wood below will be charred by the heat, and, perhaps, set on fire. The only drawback to this plan is the expense, as a great deal of gas is consumed in these stoves, and whilst we had ours at work it cost about 4d per day. It is only where gas can be obtained that this plan can be carried out, and in country places the machine must be worked by some other method. Where the machine is placed in charge of game-keepers or poultry-men who have plenty of time on their hands, the spending of an hour or two does not make any difference. We would recommend, whenever possible, that the machine be placed in charge of a woman — we use the word in its truest sense — for they have far more time and patience than we of the sterner sex. They appear to have an adeptness and art, which causes them to succeed where men fail ; in fact, they, when they take a real interest in the matter, appear to have more of the " knack" we spoke of in our first chapter. Of course, there are ladies who do not possess this " knack," and a machine is a useless thing with them. We would not, however, recommend a self-regulating machine being placed in the charge of a lady, as the delicate mechanism necessary for the regulation is — with all due deference to the fair sex — a true *bete noir* in their hands, and, unless the worker has more mechanical knowledge than is generally possessed by ladies, will be too much for them.

Many of our readers will wonder how it is that some

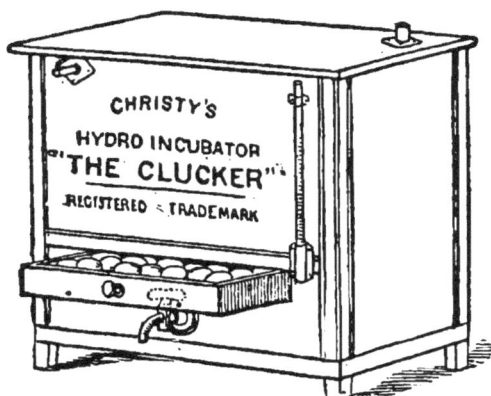

THE "CLUCKER!" HYDRO-INCUBATOR FOR 20 EGGS.

persons succeed so well, whilst others utterly fail with the same machine, both working, apparently, under the same circumstances, and the wonder is a natural one ; but we suppose it is just the same as in other matters, some have "a gift," or a plodding patience, and succeed, whilst others, under the same, or even more favorable circumstances, have to give up in despair. This will, therefore, account for the different reports given by various persons.

The merits of this machine are : its great simplicity in working ; the regularity of temperature which it keeps, caused by the fact that the lower body of water is never disturbed, and that the hot water can only mix with the cooler water gradually; the freedom from objectionable smell which all gas and oil machines give off, and which may have some injurious effect upon the imprisoned chick; and last, but not least, its reasonable price. Its defect is: The large quantity of water required to work it in cold weather ; but in spite of this, it is a very useful machine, and its introduction marks a new era in the history of artificial incubation, and we can thoroughly recommend it to any one who has the time and means of working it.

The machine used in our experiments was a 100 egg machine, which is the smallest size made, it being found that a smaller one is more affected by the temperature of the atmosphere, there not being so large a body of water, and consequently the heat is more quickly lost. Messrs. Christy make machines to hold 20, 80, and 500 eggs, and also one for ostrich eggs.

CASHMORE'S INCUBATOR.

Some readers may probably never have heard of this machine, which is the invention of Mr. Cashmore, of Loughborough, and, being sold at a very low price for a lamp machine, it may be thought to be a toy and nothing more. Such, however, is not the case, as with ordinary care and attention it will be found very useful and handy for any one who wishes to hatch only a very few birds at one time.

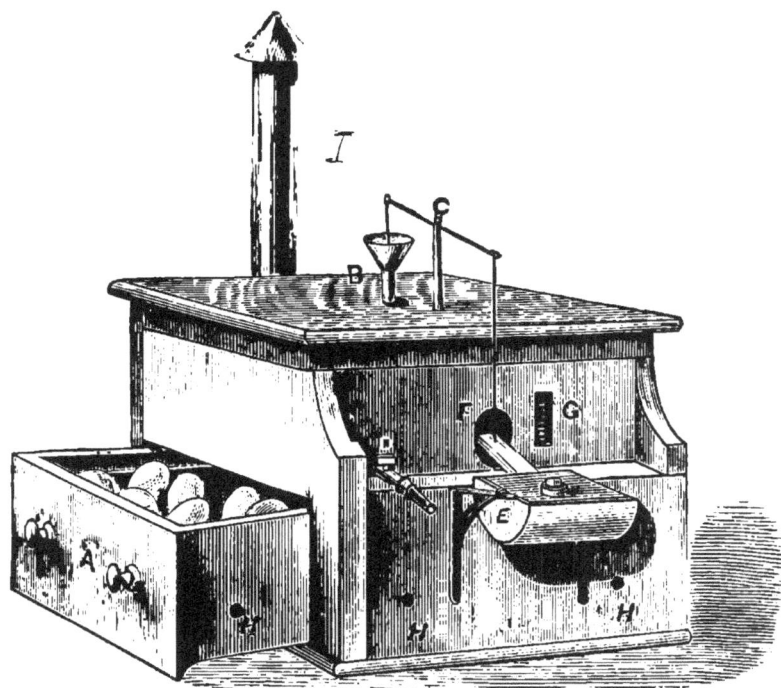

This machine stood second in the trial of incubators at Hemel Hempstead, in September last.

The machine is about 2 feet square and 18 inches high. At the front is shown the egg drawer, A, holding about 50 ordinary sized eggs, which are placed

6

upon flannel over a sheet of perforated zinc. The moisture is given from a tray not shown, which is filled with earth and kept moist, as in the Penman and Christy machines, but with the difference that it is much larger, and consequently is capable of giving off more moisture; this tray is only seen when the egg drawer is taken completely out. The inlet to the tank is at the funnel, B, which is also used for the regulator, and which we will describe presently; C is the pivot for the regulator rod; D is the exhaust pipe; E is the lamp (for benzoline), carefully balanced upon the two brackets shown in the plate; F is a tube which runs to the chimney I, and in which the burner is placed; G is the thermometer; and H are the holes for the admission of air to the eggs.

The method of working is as follows: — Hot water is poured into the funnel B until it is filled, when the machine is allowed to cool down until it comes to the requisite temperature, when the lamp is lit and fixed in position. The wire from the rod is then hooked on to the lamp, and at the other end of this rod a hollow weight is hung, which, being just balanced by the lamp, floats on the oil which is placed above the water in the funnel to prevent evaporation. Within the tube F about the quarter of an inch beyond the end of the burner, and below it, a brass tongue is placed of a wide ∧ shape inverted, and this forms the principal part of the regulator. The result is, if the machine gets hotter than the temperature at which it is set, the water in the tank naturally expands, and, having no other outlet than the funnel B, rises there, in consequence of which the weight is raised and the burner falls, cutting off nearly all the flame, and of course as soon as the temperature falls again, the water contracts, the weight is lowered, the burner rises, and the flame attains its full size. We found, when testing this machine, that it keeps its heat very even indeed, and with as much regularity as any lamp machine we have yet tried.

Considering the small size of the machine, it is wonderful how regular the heat is kept, but this is partially due to the fact that the bottom body of water is not interfered with, as the lamp heats only the upper portion. This we think a good plan, and which can be used in the gas or lamp heating machines, as well as in Hydro-Incubators. The small size and consequent cheapness is an advantage to many, who do not care to have a large and cumbersome machine, but one that they can handle easily.

The merits of this incubator are its size, the simplicity of its working, its capital regulator, its excellent arrangements for air and moisture, and the small cost for the oil it burns. Its only demerit is that the regulator will only regulate within a certain number of degrees. Our remark requires some fuller explanation to show what we mean, and it is this — that in a sudden change of temperature from, say, 50 deg. to 30 deg., the flame being full for the former, would, of itself, not be able to meet this, and the heat of the machine would go down in consequence. Again, if sudden heat came, raising the temperature of the atmosphere 20 deg., it would greatly interfere with the heat of the machine. This is, however, a matter that can always be avoided by extra attention when such occurrences take place, and is just what may be looked for in other machines more pretentious than this one.

HOWELL'S GEM HATCHER.

The "Gem" hatcher is made by Mr. F. Howell of Dunstable, a gentleman who has taken very great interest in the question of artificial incubation, and who has worked this machine very successfully. It is upon the same principle as Christy's Hydro-Incubator, and held third position in the last trial of machines at Hemel Hempstead, being scarcely 1 per cent below that of Mr. Cashmore. It is made in two sizes, namely, 60 and 100 eggs respectively, and the larger machine did the best work, the smaller machine being nearly 20 per cent below the larger one in results.

The difference between this machine and that of Messrs. Christy is the egg drawer, which is a tin tray, has very good arrangements for moisture, and the eggs are laid upon straw as in the Voitellier machine. The glass gauge which registers the height of the water is abolished, but this is a very questionable improvement, and one which might be called an improvement backward.

Mr. Howell claims that in his machines, much less water is required to work than in the Christy, and of course, this is a great advantage. It is doubtless through having a larger body of water, the larger machine holding about 25 gallons. Other than this, it is very similar to that machine.

WATSON'S "SCOTIA" INCUBATOR.

. This machine is altogether on a different principle to any other machine, being worked by lamps, but has no regulator whatever.

In appearance it is like a very flat box with one drawer in front, and an arched hole at each end of it. It is about 3 feet in length, half that width, and 15 inches in height, the outer case being wood entirely.

A tank about 1½ inches deep is fitted in it extending the whole length of the machine, holding the water, which is heated by the lamps placed in compartments of which the arched holes are the entrances. These lamps are simply ordinary paraffine lamps with the usual burners, but of course without a chimney. Above these the metal is bright, and the heat arising from the flame, which can be turned sufficiently low as not to smoke, can easily heat the water in the tank. The egg drawer is placed between the two lamp compartments, and is sufficiently large to hold 100 eggs. In the bottom of this drawer grass sods are placed, or earth, if that be more easily obtained, and kept constantly moist; above this a layer of straw is laid, on which the eggs are put. Ventilation is given over the ends and back of this drawer.

We see no reason whatever why this machine should not succeed, if kept in a proper place. It is natural to suppose that it will require more attention than either a regulating or a hot water machine, as in one there is some way of keeping the heat fairly even by means of a regulator, and in the other by the great body of water, but if kept in a room where the temperature is pretty even, we should not despair of hatching with it. Whilst believing that a few degrees variation will do no great harm, so long as the heat is not allowed to rise too much, we certainly think that the steadier the heat can be kept the better, and there is a danger now of neglecting the old desire for uniform heat, and flying to the other extreme, which must have its due attention.

The great fault in this machine is the defective ventilation. It is unwise to expect that the fresh air will run up one side, traveling over all sorts of odd corners, and finding its exit in the same manner. Some better provision ought certainly to be made, as this is one of the most important points to be attended to in all incubators, and without it, success will be ever uncertain.

The "Scotia" machine is very reasonable in price, costing only £2 10s. for a 100 egg machine.

THE VOITELLIER INCUBATOR.

This machine shares the unenviable notoriety of having completely failed at the Hemel Hempstead Tournament of Incubators in 1878, and, although previously well known, its reputation received too severe a blow to very rapidly recover a place in public estimation. Its inventor claims its principle of being a "hot nest" alone, as entirely novel in artificial hatching. In a report to the French National Academy of Agriculture, M. Joubert says, that he looks upon the Voitellier "as a true farm incubator, being as plain and durable as a plow or churn." This is true. He further says, that "the roughest-handed farm servant can take the management of it without fear of injury to its working." Be it now our duty to describe the machine and relate our experience with it, in order that our readers may, for themselves, determine how far we can indorse the latter statement.

A strong deal chest, 33 inches square and 21 inches deep, contains a cylindrical zinc cistern packed tightly round with sawdust; this hot-water tank is a foot in depth, and has 20 inches inside diameter. It exactly fits, and rests upon a circular wooden frame 4 inches in height, and this is the "hatching nest" (the English trade-mark), in which eggs are placed without any contact with the hot metal. It will hold 100 ordinary fowl eggs, or between 70 and 80 duck eggs. Two movable glazed frames, fitting the one over the other, are provided at the top of the machine, allowing either of access to the eggs when lifted off, or of a glance at the thermometer, leaning upright inside, at any time without opening. The inlet pipe is at the right hand top corner, and the only outlet tap is at the bottom. In the center of the front is a pipe to supply air, but the latter is always warmed before

being admitted to the incubator, by reason of a considerable length of the pipe running alongside of the
cistern. The air has no direct contact either with the
eggs, inasmuch as the pipe rises 9 inches inside, and a
current is secured at the top by the aid of a very
small piece of piping through which (in the published
theory) it is supposed that the steam from the hot
water escapes, and so damps the eggs sufficiently.
Suffice it here to remark, that were this the only
moisture supplied, the percentage of hatchings would
be small indeed. The cistern holds 20 gallons of
water. The nest is prepared by placing fodder, or
bracken, on a layer of sand, or gravel, an inch in
thickness. The latter is kept damp, and thus the
atmosphere in the machine should not only be always
of a proper temperature, but moist as well.

Being a hydro-incubator, the remarks upon the supply of hot water made upon the Christy machine are
equally applicable to the Voitellier. No rule can be laid
down to guide an unskilled operator in water changing,
but practice soon gives him the requisite " knack" of
telling from a glance at the thermometer how much
he will require to carry him on, either through the
day time, or night, as the case may be. In any
regular establishment for artificial incubation, where a
quantity of machines are working, and every requi-

site is to hand, with constant attention and careful supervision, of course this difficulty must be overcome entirely, and all irregularities of temperature would disappear. We are supposing that an amateur has a single machine.

Care has to be taken when the top lids are off for the purpose of attending to the eggs, that the latter are not exposed for too long a time. The inside cistern-surface is so large to come in contact with the outer air of a lower temperature, that it loses a large proportion of its heat rapidly, and when the covers are replaced, and boiling water run in, considerable time seems to elapse before the effect on the inner air is appreciable. This danger points the reader, however, to the ease with which too high a temperature is remedied. "No top contact," is M. Voitellier's principle, so that no alteration can well be made in his machine in this respect, but, in our opinion, it constitutes a danger requiring more delicate care and judgment than "the roughest-handed farm laborer" (as a rule) is possessed of. Nature is not imitated without top-contact. Here the eggs are subjected to a moist heat of 104 degs., and according as they contain germs of strong or weak constitutions, hatchings take place more or less freely.

That the Voitellier deserves a measure of success is testified to by the important results experts are claimed to have obtained with it, and we may reasonably hope that its inventor may yet prove, in an open competition, that in his hands it will perform its work as creditably as it has hitherto done in his own country. It is, in many respects, a convenient incubator; its air supply requires no regulation; its arrangements for moisture are simple and effective, apparently; its price is tolerably moderate; the thermometer can be consulted with ease and without exposing eggs; and the young chicks are provided with a nest, which seems in every way suitable to them from the moment of chipping to that of hatching out. Against these merits must be weighed the close attention it requires, as well as the large quantity of boiling water. Still if hydro-incubators are not toys, but elements of commercial enterprise, the last consideration would not be worth a thought, as proper appliances would be absolutely requisite.

BOYLE'S MACHINE.

One of the greatest difficulties that experimentalists in artificial incubation have met with has been in the regulation of heat, and until very recently it was thought that if the heat could be kept even, the whole thing was done.

The Boyle incubator is about 2 feet square and 3 feet high, having at each side a shelf with small mothers for the chickens. A door, occupying about half the entire front, on being opened displays the working apparatus, which consists of a boiler, under which room is given for the placing of the lamp or gas burner, and in front of it is fixed the regulator. Above this door are two smaller doors which open and form a slide, upon which the egg tray can rest when drawn out. These latter serve a double purpose, being in the first place the means of getting to the hatching box, which is simply a circular tray with 2 inch sides, and covered with a piece of perforated wood, in which the eggs are placed wrapped in flannel as soon as they are chipped. The doors, when open, show the bottoms of the eggs in the egg tray, and are also used for regulating the temperature at the bottom of the eggs, which is done by closing or opening them.

The hatching box is placed on the top of the boiler beneath the egg drawer. The egg tray is a perforated tray made of tin, the holes in which are about the size of an egg, but to prevent the eggs falling through, narrow strips of tin are fixed, so that the eggs are about half above and half below the tray. Upon the tray small metal cups are placed, and being kept filled with water, charge the air in the egg drawer with moisture. Above the drawer are a series of arches, under which the eggs slide, the object being to make the heat above the eggs as even as possible. The whole machine presents a neat appearance, and is finished in a first-class manner.

The most important and valuable part of the machine is the regulator.

This regulator works with the greatest nicety, and is never failing in its action. It could be left for a week without needing attention if it was set at the right temperature. We have known it work for a month with every kind of weather during that period, and the egg drawer not vary above 3 or 4 degrees, whilst the regulator will not vary half a degree. In fact, we do not know of any regulator — excepting an electric one — which we dare leave with the same confidence for any length of time. We have done some very good work, indeed, with it, hatching as far as 80 per cent of eggs placed in it, *i. e.* leaving out the unfertile and *broken* ones. We have italicized the word broken, because we wish to call special attention to what we must consider one of the defects of the machine.

There is one thing which has worked against the
success of this machine, and that is the price, considering the few eggs it holds.   The egg drawer is only
perforated for 42 eggs, and as the price is about £15
15s., only those in command of plenty of money could
afford to purchase one. We do not say for one moment
that it is too high in price considering the work there
must be in the making of it, but few people care to
spend so much for, what is to them, a thing of doubt-
ful success.

The qualities which must ever recommend this
machine are its compact form and its almost, nay
perfect, regulator.   There are several improvements
which could easily be made in it.   To our mind the
greatest defect is the egg drawer, which is both com-
plicated and useless.   If, instead of having a tray such
as it now has, it had perforated zinc, the object for
which the tray is so made, namely, the keeping cool
of the bottom of the eggs, would be gained.   The
arches under which the tray slides are also useless,
and the cause of very great annoyance and vexation.
We have had scores of eggs in various stages broken
by these arches, and often have been exasperated almost to frenzy by seeing eggs with lively and healthy
chicks in them, within a day or two of hatching,
broken in this way, and it could not be attributed to

carelessness, for if an egg was a large one, it was scarcely possible to keep it whole to the end. The hatching box is not by any means perfection, and we think the substitution of an under heat for the top heat, after the egg has chipped, tends to cramp in the chicken's legs, and to prevent weakly chicks from hatching out at all. If the egg drawer was altered, as we have suggested, there would be no need whatever for a hatching box, as a piece of flannel might be thrown over the eggs as soon as they were chipped, and would answer all the purposes required. We would also advise the keeping of a dish of water on the top of the boiler below the egg drawer, to keep the air moist. We think 102 degrees over heat, and 99 degrees under heat, the best for successful hatching with this machine.

PENMAN'S PATENT INCUBATOR.

The incubator we are about to describe was first introduced to the public two years ago, being the invention of a gentleman resident in Newcastle-upon-Tyne, who has studied the question many years, and been most successful in hatching. It won the silver medal at the Dairy Show in October, 1877, for the best incubator in action, but at the Hemel Hempstead tournament in 1878 neither of the machines sent there succeeded in hatching a single chick, although the day after the competition was over, a large number of live birds were found in the eggs.

The following is the description of the principle of the machine as taken from the prospectus:—

"It appears that every failure (in artificial incubation) must be attributed to attempts made to improve upon nature, instead of imitating her wonderful workings. In the case of the egg she has ordained the germ (so long as it is kept in a horizontal position) to float uppermost within and against the shell, in order that it may meet the genial warmth of the breast of the fowl. We must, therefore, in incubation, apply warmth to that part only, and of the degree determined by nature. A fowl of any kind prefers to incubate upon the ground. Nature having supplied the egg with only a limited quantity of moisture, has thus arranged to prevent evaporation from a large surface, as the egg is only warm at the point in contact with the fowl, until the blood vessels, searching for nourishment for the embryo, have surrounded the inner surface of the shell, when the whole egg becomes gradually warm, and eventually of an equal temperature by means of the circulation of the blood through these vessels. We must, in a word, apply the same degree of heat as nature, and in the same manner —' by top-contact' ; and, like her, allow the interior portion of the egg to remain cool, until warmed by the inward circulation of the blood. The difference between ' top-contact heat' and that received from 'radiation,' as applied to hatching, is this : by radiation, or oven heat, the eggs will be hours arriving at the desired temperature, not only when first put to hatch, but at every time afterward when they have been allowed to get cool. The egg will, of course, heat alike over its whole surface, and, consequently, evaporate equally from every part. On the contrary, heat applied in ' top-contact,' penetrates almost instantly and revivifies the germ.

" To carry out this principle, so intelligently given in the above paragraph, Mr. Cantelo, about thirty years ago, after many experiments and much consideration, found that the best way of applying the ' top-contact heat' to eggs during incubation was by a current of water flowing over an impermeable or water-proof cloth, beneath which the eggs are placed ;" and it is a pity that in the article from which the above extract is taken no reference is made to the success which he achieved.

" In constructing the incubator now brought before the public, the above principle has been constantly

kept in view and strictly carried out ; for there is no
radiating or oven heat maintained, and no egg will
be hatched in it that is not brought into top-contact
with the source of heat."

Upon the face of the matter it will be seen that this
machine, in respect to contact, is the only one which
follows nature, and there is no doubt that the
principle is a correct one, as the only heat received by
an egg from the hen is certainly where she touches it.
The difficulty which Cantelo experienced was, that
the water-proof cloth began to bag because of the
weight of water, and this, when it did so to a great
extent, crushed the eggs in the process of hatching, or
smothered the chickens as they were hatched.   He
was obliged eventually to give up the cloth, and substituted glass for it.   But his machine, like many
others, from some cause or another, passed into obliv-
ion, and only the older generation of fanciers have any
remembrance of it.

Mr. Penman, in his experiments, found that india-
rubber was the best thing he could find for his purpose, and in spite of many objections which have been
made to it, he has proved that, if properly washed before being used, all objectionable smell arising from
the sulphur is taken away.   But even india-rubber in
time bags considerably.

This incubator is made in three sizes for 50, 100 and 200 eggs respectively, the latter being the size first made.   The two larger sizes we have been very successful with, the smaller one we have never tried ourselves, although others have, but with very varying results.

The machine — we are describing the medium one — is oblong in shape, and about 30 inches high, having the appearance of a wooden frame.   In the front are seen the two trays covering the water compartment, the thermometer, the egg trays, and the mother and run ; the boiler, regulator, and lamp or gas jet, being fixed at the back.   On removing one of the trays, the india-rubber sheet, the water, and the regulation pipes immersed in the water are exposed, and the shape of the eggs, on which the rubber is lying, can be seen. The rubber is fixed into a wooden frame, and exactly midway three holes are placed, connected with a metal tube, through which the water comes after being heated in the boiler.   At each end are two holes, connected with pipes, which carries the cooler water to the mother, after which it passes to the boiler to be re-heated, so that a constant circulation is taking place. Upon the under side of this frame are fixed the egg trays, which are held in position by a wire pin and a hook.   These trays are made of zinc, with two rows

of holes for the admission of air both above and below
the eggs.   A smaller tray is fixed inside, made of perforated zinc, beneath which damp soil is placed to give
the necessary moisture.   The regulator is a very ingen-
ious contrivance, and can be made to work very effectually.   The lamp consists of a pill-box-shaped brass
vessel, upon one side of which is placed a flexible diaphragm, which, being connected by a fine rod to a
slide cut V shape, reduces the flame of the wick if
pressed over it, or if drawn back from it, allows more
flame to appear.   In the gas machine there are two
brass vessels, one of which is worked in the same manner as for lamp, but the rod is connected with the diaphragm of the opposite vessel, on the inner side of
which a fine brass pin is fixed, and which, when
pressed in, exactly fits into a fine hole, and reduces the
supply of gas (admitted by a pipe on the top) to the
burner.   In both instances the regulating power is
water or spirit, inclosed in the tubes mentioned as being seen when the tray was removed, which, having
no outlet, and being connected with the first-named
brass vessel by a small pipe, when the water expands
or contracts by the rising or falling of the heat, moves
the diaphragm, and this acts as the regulator.   It is
necessary, however, to have four or at least three of these
regulation pipes, to give a sufficient body of water or

it will not be susceptible enough. We think this was the secret of the failure of this incubator at Hemel Hempstead last year, as the machines sent there had only two tubes, and, as a consequence, the temperature was very variable. In our own experiments, we have found the same thing occur, when there were only two tubes for regulation.

The merits of this machine are, the capital arrangements for giving the necessary moisture, and the eggs being heated by actual contact. We think an improvement might be made in the fixing of the india-'rubber, as it bags very considerably after being used for a season. This could be done by fixing rods of wire below it at intervals, but there would have to be corresponding partitions in the egg trays, to prevent the eggs from touching and being broken by these wires. It would also be an advantage to do away with the mother altogether, as it is too boxed up, or to make it more open, and to close in the sides and front of the machine, as the egg trays are too much exposed, for in very cold weather the eggs are chilled when against the sides of the trays. If these improvements were made, and four tubes used for the regulator, it would be a very good and useful machine.

Its success at the autumn show of the Northumberland Agricultural Society and the Dairy Show held at

Islington, London, in 1877, were severe tests, for at the latter eggs were taken in process of incubation from Newcastle to London, and there hatched in the Agricultural Hall. In conclusion, we may say that for a perfect regulating and working incubator, we should think Boyle's regulator and Penman's incubator would be unequaled.

From the foregoing pages, our readers can obtain a very correct idea of the progress made in England in this specialty, and by comparison can readily see how far we are in advance of our English cousins.

CHAPTER X.

ARTIFICIAL MOTHERS.

" Foster mothers" they might well be called, and the experience of many breeders has been that they are much to be preferred to the hen. They are a very useful appendage to the poultry yard in more ways than one, even though you may not use an incubator.

The hen has enjoyed her needed rest from her ordinary duties of laying, while employed for three weeks in hatching the eggs — and now the young chicks when twenty-four hours old can be removed to the artificial mother, and the hen, returned to the laying house, to again resume her usual duties.

In the artificial mother it is a much easier task to feed and care for the young chicks, and to protect them from vermin and rats, the scourges of the poultry-yard. The chickens are completely under your control, and are not being tramped to death by some booted Mongolian, or picked to death by the ferocious game, into whose coop the unfortunate little fellow may have accidentally strayed.

If you are rearing chickens upon a large scale, the mothers will be found to be almost an absolute necessity, and extensive breeders who have used them, are of the opinion that the artificial is to be preferred to the natural hen.   They are certainly a great economizer of labor and time, and many things can be said in their favor.   For their use, there should be a proper house provided, with light ventilation, and in cold or damp weather, the proper heat and temperature should be maintained by use of a small stove; keep a dry atmosphere, avoid draughts, and success can be readily attained in raising fine, healthy chicks.

The use of artificial mothers has answered the inquiry often made, as to how we shall rear the young chicks after they are hatched out, for success as much depends upon successfully rearing them, as any thing else.

Another question often asked, is, how do they learn to eat?   An easy matter, surely; if they do not readily eat when twenty-four hours old, one or two chickens somewhat older can be placed with them, and they will readily learn.

CHAPTER XI.

CARE OF THE CHICKS.

It seems to be an easy thing to bring the little fellows into existence; and the question then arises, how shall we care for them, and successfully rear them? In this, as well as in incubation, common sense is a desideratum. Much thought and labor have been devoted to this subject for many years by men of practical experience; and various devices have been invented to protect and care for the chicks, some of which we have described in the previous pages. The young chicks should be removed from the incubator to the brooder when from twelve to fifteen hours old, and then require their first feed, which should be composed of hard-boiled eggs, bread crumbs, wet up with a little milk. Even if their first feed is delayed a few hours longer it will not be at all prejudicial to their welfare. We have many inquiries asking how we shall learn them to eat; to such, we say, it any thing is "natural" in this world, it is the knowledge

all animals have, of " how to eat." As the chicks grow
and thrive they should be provided with as varied a
diet as possible, and fed at regular intervals, and as
often as circumstances will permit. If it can be
arranged for the first few weeks, the following would
be a good schedule: five, nine, twelve, A. M., three,
six and nine, P. M., and if they can have a feed later
than that, at night, so much the better. Early chickens
are very important to all poultry-keepers, and in no way
can they be so well secured as by giving every possible
care to the way in which they are fed and managed,
from the time they leave the shell, until they are fit
for broilers, or able to care for themselves. The simplicity and certainty with which these results can be
accomplished is apparent to those who have given the
subject any study at all. If the chicks are confined
to the brooder and dry runs, they should be provided
with grain food; and as soon as old enough should be
allowed a grass run. But be sure that it is protected
against rats, cats, hawks and the various enemies of the
poultry yard. Lettuce chopped fine is the best substitute
for green grass, and young cabbage sprouts, chopped
onions and potato mash have always been very valuable.

Milk is one of the most beneficial things that can
possibly be fed to chickens, young or old; and they

cannot have too much of it, though it should not be given them to the exclusion of water. In the early spring months it will be found very desirable to warm the milk that is given to them, especially if early in the morning; it will serve as an excellent stimulant.

The longer the little attentions we have named can be continued to them, the better they will thrive and the greater will be the results that will be attained. As soon as they begin to relish it, finely-chopped meat will also prove very beneficial to them, and conducive to their growth and stamina of constitution. As they grow up, the dry grains should be substituted as rapidly as possible for the wet food, and it will do much to prevent gapes, and a dozen little ailments that chicken flesh is heir to. A good rule to observe in feeding them is to only give them, each time, just what they will eat up clean, and keep their appetites good, and thus prevent them from getting cloyed on any kind of food. A requisite in the raising of chickens is dry quarters; dampness in any form they cannot stand, and care and judgment should be exercised in this particular. Better not attempt to do any thing if you are to leave it half done, and better not attempt to rear chickens unless you have a suitable place for them, and are prepared to give them the care and attention that they will most certainly demand. Not the slightest difficulty need be experienced in the rearing of chickens artificially, if you will only give it proper thought, attention and common sense. That it is economy, none can question ; time is saved in feeding, time is saved in care, and the life of many a luckless chick saved from the heavy feet of the mother, and dozens of similar causes. That they are being more and more used each year is plainly apparent to all who have made the subject a study, and that incubators and brooders are revolutionizing the poultry interests is no longer a question.

DISEASES, PREVENTION AND CURE.

Few diseases occur where the proper precautions are used ; and they are generally produced by cold, dampness, filth or want of care.

DIARRHŒA is caused by just the things we have noted, it can usually be checked by giving boiled rice, with which a little powdered chalk has been mixed. Give a little cayenne pepper in their food, and add a few drops of camphor to their drinking water.

CRAMPS. Remove to a thoroughly dry warm place and bathe their limbs with Pond's Extract, which we have found to be a valuable auxiliary to the poultryman's medicine chest.

GAPES. These are caused by small worms lodging in the wind-pipe. They may often be removed by use of a horse-hair loop, and often may be destroyed by using a few drops of kerosene oil (use sparingly) or by giving a little camphor, or ammonia spirits in their drinking water. They rarely trouble chicks properly cared for.

LICE. Dozens of remedies are given to both prevent and kill lice. One of the oldest we know of has proved the best : sulphur and lard, carefully used, and kerosene freely applied to roosts and coops.

PIP. This is a horny scale that appears on the tip of the tongue. It may be carefully removed with the finger-nail or pen-knife, and is generally caused by some stoppage of the breathing apparatus of nose or head, causing a dryness in the throat. A wash of "Labbaraque's Solution," which can be procured of any druggist, will be found very beneficial. Chickens affected with it will be readily detected by their difficulty of breathing, causing a piping, wheezing noise, and it is often accompanied with a cold, feverish symptoms and foul breath, and may be taken for something worse than it really is.

ROUP in young chicks is seldom any thing else than a severe cold, and many of the harsh remedies that are resorted to should be deprecated. It is usually known by a discharge from the nostrils, eyes, and fetid smell from throat. A wash of vinegar, diluted, is good, and some simple pill of camphor, ammonia, etc., such as are sold by all dealers in poultry supplies, will be found efficacious. We have a drawer full of letters sent to us by Miller & Co., of Plainfield, N. J., from scores of breeders who have used their "Sure Cure Roup Pills" with great success. Among the letters we recognize the familiar autographs of many prominent breeders and we feel justified in strongly recommending the medicine to those who may need a remedy of the kind. The formula they use is one that has been used successfully for years in England and France, and unhesitatingly indorsed by the fraternity.

I. K. FELCH,

Light Brahmas, Plymouth Rocks,

DARK BRAHMAS, P. COCHINS,

Leghorns & B. B. R. G. Bantams,

AND

SHEPHERD DOGS.

- - - - - - - -

READ!

The Felch Pedigree LIGHT BRAHMAS exhibited in 19 Exhibitions the past show season, had a possible chance to win 93 Prizes—they won 84 Prizes. This has never been done by any other Strain in America.

NATICK, MASS.

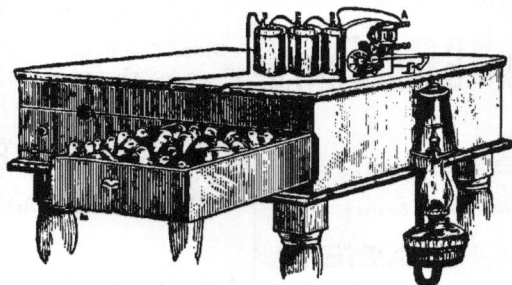

www.ingramcontent.com/pod-product-compliance
Lightning Source LLC
Chambersburg PA
CBHW030609270326
41927CB00007B/1103